SOARING
ON HIGH

SOARING ON HIGH

SPIRITUAL INSIGHTS FROM THE LIFE OF AN EAGLE

MARY WHELCHEL

MOODY PRESS
CHICAGO

All Scripture quotations, unless otherwise indicated, are taken from the *Holy Bible, New International Version*®. NIV®. Copyright © 1973, 1978, 1984 by International Bible Society. Used by permission of Zondervan Publishing House. All rights reserved.

Scripture quotations marked NASB are taken from the *New American Standard Bible*®, © Copyright The Lockman Foundation 1960, 1962, 1963, 1968, 1971, 1972, 1973, 1975, 1977, 1995. Used by permission.

Scripture quotations marked PHILLIPS: Reprinted with permission of Scribner, a Division of Simon & Schuster, from THE NEW TESTAMENT IN MODERN ENGLISH, Revised Edition, translated by J. B. Phillips. Copyright © 1958, 1960, 1972 by J. B. Phillips.

Scripture quotations marked (KJV) are taken from the King James Version.

Library of Congress Cataloging-in-Publication Data

Whelchel, Mary
  Soaring on high : spiritual insights from the life of the eagle / Mary Whelchel.
    p. cm.
  Includes bibliographical references.
  ISBN 0-8024-1788-4
  1. Spiritual life--Christianity. 2. Eagles--Religious aspects--Christianity. I. Title.

BV4501.2 . W4395 2001
248.4--dc21

2001030092

3 5 7 9 10 8 6 4

Printed in the United States of America

To Claudia
who is soaring like an eagle
in the midst of a difficult storm

CONTENTS

INTRODUCTION

My interest in eagles began some years ago when I heard a sermon that stirred my curiosity. Until then I had given little thought to eagles, but the message touched a chord in my heart and that caused me to begin to research this unique bird. From that came a message of my own, which I presented on my radio program as well as to many groups across the country.

I was amazed at the response to this message. It seemed that everyone related to eagles, wanted to know more about them, and gained valuable insight for their own lives from the eagle. Almost every time I talked about eagles, someone in the audience would give me additional information or stories about eagles to add to my knowledge and my message.

People requested copies of the message to share with their children because they knew it would be of interest to young people as well. As I applied the story of eagles to our everyday lives, I saw how God used it to teach truth that can transform people and give them renewed hope and encouragement.

At one of these events a woman asked me if I had written a book about eagles. Her question made me think that perhaps such a book would be helpful. And you now have that book in your hands.

What I have learned since beginning this eagles' exploration of my own is that, like no other bird, eagles hold a special place in the minds of people all over the world. I've talked about eagles in Kenya and Kazakhstan and Switzerland and Canada, as well as many of our U.S. states, and the eagle never fails to communicate, even across cultural and language barriers. Almost everybody relates to eagles and wants to hear more about them. Like many others, I have begun collecting eagle statues. An eagle in flight sits on my desk all the time, and I never tire of looking at the beauty and grandeur of this marvelous creature.

THE KING OF BIRDS

For centuries, the eagle has been recognized by many nations, kingdoms, and empires as the "King of Birds." This majestic bird has become an international symbol of freedom, strength, immortality, and authority.

In America the bald eagle is the national emblem, officially declared so by the Second Continental Congress in 1782. It has come to represent the spirit of freedom that characterizes our country and the strength of character and excellence to which we aspire. You will find references to the eagle abundant in our art, folklore, music, and architecture.

But long before the United States recognized the eagle, the writers of the Bible referred to eagles as illustrations and examples to communicate their message. Obviously, eagles were well known and recognized thousands of years ago, and the esteem and fascination we feel for eagles today began with time itself. God created eagles in a very special way, and their beauty and characteristics have brought much enjoyment and beauty into our lives.

THE EAGLE IN SCRIPTURE

The Bible has over twenty-five specific references to eagles. No other bird has that much ink in Scripture, which sends a message about its prominence among birds. The most famous scriptural reference to eagles is the passage from Isaiah 40:31: "But those who hope in the LORD will renew their strength. They will soar on wings like eagles; they will run and not grow weary, they will walk and not be faint."

We've quoted it and sung it many times; it's a verse which we all love because of the imagery of soaring like eagles. Soaring above the clouds. Nothing keeping us down. Freedom from cares and struggles. Power to rise above the difficulties of life. Strength to keep going no matter what. Never being bound by earthly things. Who doesn't want to soar!

Could that be the main purpose God created the eagle as He did—to give us this awesome picture of soaring to which we can aspire? To inspire us through the eagle to never be satisfied with "earthboundedness"? Perhaps He placed in us this instinctive fascination for this bird so that we would listen well and learn the lessons He wanted to teach us through the eagle.

WHICH BIRD DO YOU RESEMBLE?

Let's face it—there are other birds to which we have a more natural likeness. For example, there's the canary, a beautiful little bird that is content to sing all day in a cage. Never soars; has to be fed by others; has no power or authority in its wings. That describes me all too often. I can be too easily contented with chirping away in my own confined, comfortable world, never trying my wings to discover the joy of soaring.

Then there are the buzzards. There's nothing beautiful about these birds. They are content to sit on telephone poles and squawk, looking for dead things to eat. They have no beautiful song, and they don't know how to soar. Sometimes I find myself sitting on the sidelines, complaining, criticizing, judging, instead of soaring. I wonder if I look like a buzzard to God sometimes.

What about the peacock—there's a beautiful bird, for sure. Colorful and big. But this bird is extremely self-focused, preens all the time, struts around to show off its beautiful feathers, and is terribly self-important. But you'll never see a peacock soaring above the clouds!

God must surely look down from heaven and see me at times behaving like a peacock instead of soaring like an eagle. How preoccupied I can be with myself; how important I can think I am; how self-involved I can become.

God wants us to soar like eagles. We don't have to settle for cages or telephone poles or beauty parades. We have the incredible opportunity to learn how to soar like eagles, and when we fall short of that, we miss out on many wonderful things God has planned for us.

THERE'S MORE TO SOARING
THAN MEETS THE EYE

When you study the eagle, you discover that there is much more to an eagle's life than the effortless soaring that has become its identifying feature. Before an eagle soars, he has to learn some difficult lessons. And the eagle's existence is often filled with troubles, hard work, difficult circumstances, unpleasant environments, discouragement, and failure.

Sound familiar? There are many parallels between the life of an eagle and our own. For us to soar like an eagle, we have to know how to deal with the currents of our lives. We have to learn how to soar and be willing to leave our feathered nests. We have to develop effective launching pads that allow us to catch God's currents, and we have to know how our strength can be renewed, like the eagle's.

What I hope to accomplish in this book is to introduce you to some of the characteristics of eagles and how they live, and through their example to encourage you to set your sights on soaring. I hope you will become unhappy with anything less than soaring and that you will learn some new, practical ways to soar. There is much we can learn from the eagle so that we can be "more than conquerors through him who loved us" (Romans 8:37).

So, if you're up to learning how to soar, join me as we look at the eagle and see why God chose this bird as a beautiful teaching example and role model for us.

THE UNIQUE EAGLE DESIGN

As a teenager I wanted to be like everyone else. It's a typical teenage malady—this obsessive need to conform, to be accepted, to blend in. In those young years the worst thing that can happen to you is to draw attention to yourself because you're weird, or nerdy, or . . . oh, no . . . different! Some people never get over that phase in their lives, but thankfully most of us are able to move on and learn to be ourselves.

I remember that one of my biggest concerns was my feet. I wore size nine shoes when everyone else was wearing fives and sixes. Do you know how it feels as a girl to have big feet when you're in high school? It can be traumatic.

I used to daydream about having small feet and being able to walk into a shoe store and say, "Size six, please." I seriously considered cutting off my toes—provided I could still walk afterwards and could talk my parents into it. I lay awake at night wondering if there was a footlift operation of some kind for people who wanted to change the size of their feet.

We typically don't like to be different. But if we want to soar like eagles, we must first accept the fact that eagles are different from other birds, and we'll have to be willing to be different, too. You can't soar with ordinary wings. It takes extraordinary and unique wings, such as eagles have.

Even great, wise Solomon admitted that the way an eagle soars in the sky is amazing and hard to understand. He wrote: "There are three things that are too amazing for me, four that I do not understand: the way of an eagle in the sky . . ." (Proverbs 30:18–19). Solomon was so taken with the way eagles soared that they topped his list of things that were too amazing for him to understand.

EAGLES ARE BUILT DIFFERENTLY

Bald eagles are unique to North America, whereas the golden eagle can be found not only in North America, but in parts of Europe and Asia as well as northern Africa. Though they are different in coloring, the bald eagle and golden eagle are similar in size and build. Typically these eagles have a six- to seven-foot wing span and weigh up to fifteen pounds.

The design of their wings makes them aerodynamically superior to other birds. Each wing has more than 1,250 feathers, which are separated at the tips like the fingers of a hand. When the eagle spreads those huge wings and the multitudinous feathers spread their fingertips, he is able to catch the current of the wind and soar like no other bird ever has.

EAGLES FLY HIGH AND FAST

Because of their unique wing structure, eagles soar higher than any other bird. They soar effortlessly at altitudes of over ten thousand feet and can stay aloft for hours because of their ability to ride the currents and catch thermal updrafts.

In addition, they are able to fly at remarkable speeds. They've been clocked at over 65 miles per hour in level flight, and 150 to 200 miles per hour when they're in a full dive.

THE EAGLE ADVANTAGE

The unique design of eagles gives them a remarkable advantage in many ways. For example, they can build their nests at much higher elevations than can other birds, giving them a strategic vantage point that gives them greater protection. These locations also provide a launching pad for flight, allowing them to take advantage of the wind currents at high altitude. The eagle's ability to fly fast also allows it to attack a prey or a predator with its beaks and talons with the force of a bullet. In addition, it can fly for long periods without becoming exhausted, because its unique wings allow it to soar on the wind current, with very little flapping required. The eagle can actually rest and relax as it soars because it doesn't have to flap its wings.

WE, TOO, ARE DIFFERENT

As God's chosen people we, like the eagle, are structured differently. I certainly don't mean to imply that Christians are to be weird or strange, but being born into God's family gives us different wings, if you please. We get a sense of this uniqueness that is ours as we listen to our Lord praying to His Father for us: "My prayer is not that you take them out of the world but that you protect them from the evil one. They are not of the world, even as I am not of it" (John 17:15–16).

Jesus stated this as a fact: those who are His disciples through saving faith are not of this world. We don't have an option here; that's the way it is.

What does it mean to be "not of this world"? It certainly doesn't mean that we don't live in this world any longer, nor does it mean that Christians should be isolated. We don't need and shouldn't have Christian communes where we surround ourselves only with other Christians and screen out the world as much as possible. Jesus clearly wants us to be in this world, but not of it.

I've spent some time in foreign countries. I never became a citizen of those countries, but I lived there and functioned there. I learned to adapt myself as necessary to their culture in order to survive, but I was never "one of them," if you please. I was *in* the country but not *of* it.

Similarly, we are *in* this world—this foreign country for us Christians—but we are not *citizens* of it. We don't exchange our Christian culture and principles for that of the world's. We learn how to adapt as necessary to this world without being like it.

Peter wrote:

> But you are a chosen people, a royal priesthood, a holy nation, a people belonging to God, that you may declare the praises of him who called you out of darkness into his wonderful light. Once you were not a people, but now you are the people of God; once you had not received mercy, but now you have received mercy. (1 Peter 2:9–10)

There is a reason that Jesus wants us to be in this world but not of it. It is so that we can declare the praises of Him who has changed us, who has given us eagle's wings. We have one reason for being left here on earth in this world of which we are no longer citizens, and that is to bring praise and glory to our Lord Jesus Christ. That's our reason for living here. Otherwise we would be far better off to go right home to heaven as soon as we're born into the family of God.

So, we're in this world but not of it. Now we have eagle's wings and we can soar. That's because we become new persons once we become believers in Jesus Christ. Paul wrote to the Corinthians: "Therefore, if anyone is in Christ, he is a new creation; the old has gone, the new has come!" (2 Corinthians 5:17).

DO YOU HAVE YOUR WINGS YET?

Maybe this is a good time to ask the question: Have you been made a new creation in Christ? This book is about setting your sights on soaring, but that can't happen if you don't have your "eagle's wings." What does a person have to do to become this new creation in Christ and acquire those wings that will allow him to soar? Well, the Bible is clear on this.

> That if you confess with your mouth, "Jesus is Lord," and believe in your heart that God raised him from the dead, you will be saved. For it is with your heart that you believe and are justified, and it is with your mouth that you confess and are saved. . . . "Everyone who calls on the name of the Lord will be saved." (Romans 10:9–10, 13)

There must be a point in your life where you recognize clearly that you have a serious sin problem and you cannot personally do anything about it. It's bigger than you are! You can't be good enough to earn God's salvation, no matter how hard you try.

At that point, fully aware of your need, you must confess your sinful nature and your sinful past, ask for the forgiveness that comes through Jesus Christ, believe in your heart that Jesus has provided salvation for you through His death and resurrection, and then proclaim your faith in Jesus Christ by testifying with your mouth.

You could do that right now, where you are, with a simple prayer of confession. If you need further guidance or have unanswered questions, you should find a qualified friend or pastor who can take the Bible and give you additional insight into God's free gift of salvation, which is offered to you.

If there is no one in your life to give you that kind of help, you are welcome to call a hotline that is there to help in these situations. You call 1-888-NEED HIM. Jesus said that if you seek, you will find. Please make sure this issue is firmly and completely settled in your mind. Until you get your eagle's wings, soaring like an eagle will just not be possible.

LIFE WITH NEW WINGS

Once you are born from above, made a new creation in Christ, you have what it takes to soar because you have your wings. Life changes for you. You sense a freedom and joy that wasn't there before. It is as though some huge weight has been lifted from your shoulders and, more importantly, from your heart. The cloud of guilt that always hung over your head has evaporated.

This is how the apostle Paul expressed it, and it's one of my favorite verses in all the Bible: "Therefore, there is now no condemnation for those who are in Christ Jesus, because through Christ Jesus the law of the Spirit of life set me free from the law of sin and death" (Romans 8:1).

You know, the whole world is obsessed with freedom. Everybody wants to be free, but not many people know true freedom. When you get your eagle's wings, you are really free. Free from the law of sin and death, free from the penalty of eternity in hell, free from the bondage to sin that held you so firmly in its grasp.

Our country was founded on freedom—freedom of speech, freedom of the press, freedom of religion, freedom to pursue happiness—and we are passionate about our freedoms. Thank God for the privilege of living in a country that holds to these basic human freedoms and liberties.

However, none of those freedoms truly makes you free. If you're still in bondage to sin, freedom of speech doesn't really help that much. If you can't get rid of guilt, freedom to pursue happiness is an empty phrase because you can't find happiness with that cloud over your head.

But with your eagle's wings, you are now truly free. You could be locked in a prison and still be free because you are free inside, and there's nothing to compare with that freedom. To the Galatians Paul wrote: "It is for freedom that Christ has set us free. Stand firm, then, and do not let yourselves be burdened again by a yoke of slavery" (Galatians 5:1).

Like a bird out of a cage, we've been released to soar like eagles. Released from the slavery of sin, from the condemnation we deserve, from the penalty that hung over our heads. Released—let out of our prisons of sin—to fly high!

THE CHRISTIAN'S ADVANTAGE

Just because we are members of God's family, born again through faith in Jesus Christ, we have many advantages, not unlike those of the eagle. These advantages are ours by inheritance. We can take no credit for them because they are gifts from our heavenly Father.

WE CAN FLY HIGH!

Like eagles, as believers in Jesus Christ we are intended to fly at very high altitudes—in the heavenlies:

> And God raised us up with Christ and seated us with him in the heavenly realms in Christ Jesus, in order that in the coming ages he might show the incomparable riches of his grace, expressed in his kindness to us in Christ Jesus. (Ephesians 2:6–7)

We are made for heavenly realms. Notice that this is in the present tense, not the future tense. Sure, we'll dwell with the Lord in heaven for all eternity, but we have the privilege of soaring in heavenly realms even while residing on this earth.

Are you thinking: *There are no heavenly realms where I live!* I know the feeling. You look around you and see evil and trouble and sorrow and broken relationships and pain. Surely this is not heavenly realms.

What does it mean that we are even now seated with Christ in heavenly realms? It means that is our position because of Christ. That is how God sees us because we've been born into His family. With the eternal God there is no future or past; everything is present time. So He declares that we are even now in those heavenly realms.

Our new nature, with these eagle's wings, makes us want to soar up high, close to Christ, in heavenly realms. We know from what Jesus taught us that we are still in this world, but we are not to be of it. Therefore, He gives us eagle's wings so that we are capable of living above the evil and dirt and depression of this world.

Here's how that works in everyday life. You go to a job where the name of Jesus is mostly a curse word. You look around you and see a total disregard for God and His principles. You talk to people who never give God a thought, if they believe in Him at all. You watch those you love making choices to live sinful lives and turn their backs on the God of the Bible. And the dirt of the world seems to infect you, discourage you, and even attract you at times.

But you remember that you've got eagle's wings, and through prayer and a refocusing of your mind, you take advantage of your position. You've been cleared to soar in heavenly realms, and so in the midst of that degenerate and evil environment, you take off. You offer your body as a living sacrifice and you are transformed by the renewing of your mind (Romans 12:1–2). That transformation allows you to soar above the circumstances of your life, the evil of your society, and the dirt of your world.

You soar up to those heavenly realms where you can have instant and constant fellowship with God through Jesus Christ. The world around you may not even be aware that you've just taken off and left it in the dust, but you know it. You know that you are in that heavenly realm where Jesus is Lord and the purity and joy and truth of that heavenly altitude floods your mind and your soul with peace.

You look at the people around you who are still earthbound, and your heart is touched by their plight because you realize they don't have wings to soar. They're stuck in that evil place, but you are free. The world cannot hold you on the ground any longer. You've got your wings, and you can soar higher and higher because you're on the wings of an eagle.

This ability to fly high gives you more than just freedom. It gives you a unique perspective of the world beneath you. You look at everything very differently when you see it from heavenly realms, and you realize how distorted your priorities and concerns were when you were earthbound.

Eagle's wings allow you to soar high enough to get God's bird's-eye view of the world, your problems, your life, and others. That heavenly soaring changes your priorities and puts new paradigms into your everyday life, and you see people and things much differently than ever before.

Once you've tasted the freedom of soaring on eagle's wings into the heavenly realms, you'll never be satisfied with cages or telephone poles or beauty parades. Nothing compares to the blessedness of soaring higher and higher.

The end result of soaring in heavenly realms in Christ Jesus is that it allows us the opportunity to demonstrate the astonishing grace of God. As Paul wrote, we are in those heavenly realms "in order that in the coming ages he might show the incomparable riches of his grace, expressed in his kindness to us in Christ Jesus" (Ephesians 2:7).

Soaring is not all about us—about our freedom, our abilities, or our performance. It is not to bring attention to ourselves or to make us feel good about ourselves. Soaring in heavenly realms is all about God, so that those who are still earthbound can see what God's grace can do.

The very idea that we can soar like an eagle—go figure! How could it be? We know, and others do as well, that we could never soar on our own. We know how inadequate we were before we got our wings. And now, as proof of God's grace so freely given to unworthy people, we soar higher and higher in order that His grace can be demonstrated in the world around us.

Yes, we are built to fly high, in heavenly realms. There's no need to settle for anything less!

WE CAN SOAR FOR LONG PERIODS

Endurance and perseverance are two virtues that are not that prominent in our culture today. Enduring and persevering take time; they often mean postponed gratification and enjoyment; they require patience and denial of oneself. But one of our unique advantages as believers in Jesus Christ, with our new eagle's wings, is that we can keep on keepin' on when it looks like mission impossible. That's because we can soar on the winds.

Wind is often used in Scripture to describe the Holy Spirit. In explaining the new birth to Nicodemus, Jesus said: "You should not be surprised at my saying, 'You must be born again.' The wind blows wherever it pleases. You hear its sound, but you cannot tell where it comes from or where it is going. So it is with everyone born of the Spirit" (John 3:7–8).

On the day of Pentecost, the Spirit of God descended on the disciples like wind:

> When the day of Pentecost came, they were all together in one place. Suddenly a sound like the blowing of a violent wind came from heaven and filled the whole house where they were sitting. They saw what seemed to be tongues of fire that separated and came to rest on each of them. All of them were filled with the Holy Spirit and began to speak in other tongues as the Spirit enabled them. (Acts 2:1–4)

And even angels are described as winds: "In speaking of the angels he says, 'He makes his angels winds, his servants flames of fire'" (Hebrews 1:7).

With our eagle's wings and the winds provided by our heavenly Father, we too can soar for long periods, enduring and persevering in the face of what looks like impossible odds. Notice Paul's parting words to the Christians in Rome:

> For everything that was written in the past was written to teach us, so that through endurance and the encouragement of the Scriptures we might have hope.
>
> May the God who gives endurance and encouragement give you a spirit of unity among yourselves as you follow Christ Jesus, so that with

one heart and mouth you may glorify the God and Father of our Lord
Jesus Christ. (Romans 15:4–6)

In one of his great prayers for his children in Christ, Paul prayed:

And we pray this in order that you may live a life worthy of the Lord
and may please him in every way: bearing fruit in every good work, growing in the knowledge of God, being strengthened with all power according to his glorious might so that you may have great endurance and
patience, and joyfully giving thanks to the Father, who has qualified
you to share in the inheritance of the saints in the kingdom of light.
(Colossians 1:10–12)

It may not be the best grammatical construction you've ever read,
but packed in that two-verse sentence is some important theology. It
reminds me again that everything in my life should be all about God,
not all about me. Paul is praying for his friends, asking that they will
have great spiritual knowledge, wisdom, and understanding, not so that
their self-esteem will improve, but so that they may live a worthy life
and please God. Then he lists what is worthy and what will please God:

- "bearing fruit in every good work"
- "growing in the knowledge of God"
- "being strengthened with all power according to his glorious
  might so that you may have great endurance and patience"
- "joyfully giving thanks to the Father"

Imagine all the Christians you know *bearing fruit in every good
work.* That would mean that we'd have more Christians involved in
ministry instead of being spectators.

Have you noticed our tendency to look for Christian entertainment rather than asking God where He wants to use our gifts and in
what body of believers He needs our talents? The entertainment culture has permeated our Christian lifestyle, and, as a result, many believers never develop or use their gifts in the body of Christ, as is the
purpose for their gifts. Our church and ministry programs often limp
along, or we have a few exhausted people trying to carry the whole load.

We will be *growing in our knowledge of God.* Ask yourself, Do I know God better today than a year ago? It takes time and commitment to get to know God, as it does anyone else, but it will be a trademark of a maturing Christian.

Then, Paul prays that the Colossians *will have power to endure and be patient.* He knows that the road will not always be easy or fun or exciting. He knows that discouragement and frustration will frequently fly in their faces. But he also knows that when they are strengthened with God's power, they can endure with patience.

That's what we can do when we soar on the winds. We stretch out those special wings that are ours because of faith in Jesus Christ, and we let the wind of God's Spirit carry us. And with His wind under our wings, we can endure.

There are thousands and thousands of illustrations of this in the lives of many believers throughout the ages. From Job to the apostles of old, to Amy Carmichael, to Corrie ten Boom, we have examples of those who have endured.

I think of a woman who displayed incredible endurance in the face of many health problems. You would not recognize her name. She did not win any earthly fame, though she accomplished a great deal during her lifetime. She was a single woman in her eighties when she recently died; her fiancé was killed in the Second World War, and she chose not to marry after that. She prayed for me and my ministry every day for at least fifteen years. She encouraged me and cheered me on more times than I can recall. She was in constant twenty-four-hour-a-day pain for the last months of her life, and no amount of doctors and specialists could find the right combination of treatments and medicines to give her any relief. I told God often that I didn't understand why she had to suffer so. Why her, of all people?

Though frequently she could hardly lift her head, she never complained. She just kept on enduring, trusting in the God whose methods she didn't understand. She had great endurance and patience. Those eagle's wings carried her when nothing else could. She continued to stretch out those wings and let the wind of God's Spirit and her knowledge of God's Word carry her.

Why are so many Christians quitters instead of soarers? Because they are not flying high enough to catch the powerful winds of God's Spirit. They haven't taken advantage of their eagle attributes, and they aren't behaving like eagles at all but more like the canaries and buzzards and peacocks of the world.

The Spirit-filled life is unknown to all too many of us who are truly born into God's family. We keep trying to do everything on our own, or we refuse to do what is necessary for high flying. So we never really catch the winds that should be carrying us, and we never learn to endure with patience.

LET GO OF WHAT WEIGHS YOU DOWN

With its huge talons, an eagle is capable of grabbing a very large fish or animal for dinner. Diving down at those incredible speeds, he spots that big fish swimming near the surface, or that rabbit he can see as far as a mile away, and grabs it with both talons, then begins to climb up and away, taking dinner home for the family.

However, if his eyes are bigger than his stomach, and that fish or animal is too heavy for him, the eagle may drown or be dashed to the ground because he won't let go once he has latched on to his prey. The very skill he is so well-gifted to do can become his tragic end if he doesn't know when to let go.

If we want to soar like eagles, we have to learn when to let go. This hits me between the eyes. I'm not a "let-goer." It is against my nature. I am a "hanger-oner." I like ribbons tied on all my packages, nothing left undone, nothing dangling, neat little ends to every story. But life doesn't work that way, and if we don't know when and how to let go, we can drown in our own stubbornness.

At one time in my life there was a woman I tried to help. I truly went out of my way to give her a "leg up," if you please, and I thought I was doing it for the right reasons and with the right motives. But as the months ticked off, she became a burden, a puzzle, and a weight around my neck, and nothing I did improved the relationship. I could never please her, and in spite of all my efforts, she didn't seem to be making any progress toward putting her past behind her and going forward to what God had for her in the future. She continued to be mired in her past, and it felt like she was pulling me into that sinking sand with her.

Naturally, I thought it was my fault. Guilt comes easy to me, and if something is wrong, my first assumption is that I'm to blame. That's probably because I often *am* to blame, but in this case I took on false guilt! The more I failed at solving this relationship problem, the harder I tried to fix it. I just couldn't believe that with good motives and much effort I couldn't "turn this thing around" and have a success story. I could imagine telling how God had transformed her—and what a glorious illustration that would be for many messages and books!

For a couple of long years I kept hanging on. But like the eagle who won't let go, I began to drown in this relationship. It was affecting my ministry, my peace, my effectiveness, and other relationships, and I could see nothing good happening as a result.

Finally God brought a person into my life who, in one brief conversation, helped me open my eyes and recognize the truth about the relationship. This man never knew what he did for me, for he had no knowledge of this other person, but in the course of a conversation, he explained how some people find their identity in martyrdom and victimization, and if they aren't currently being mistreated, they will make it up. In one moment I understood what was happening, and finally I let go.

I was able to leave that relationship without a bow on the package. I don't have a glorious story to tell you of the woman's transformation. As far as I know, she has continued in the same pattern, and it even seems to have gotten worse. I have no doubt that God's power can change her, if she is ever willing to allow Him to do that. But I know that I can't change her, no matter how much I try.

I learned an important "let-go" lesson in that relationship. I can so well remember the freedom I felt as I walked away from this dear man, with the blinders off my eyes, and said to the Lord, "I'm letting go without a bow on this package, and it's OK." The sense of failure was lifted, and I was free again to soar.

Perhaps women are more prone to hang on than men because of our nurture nature and our desire to make everybody happy. But I'm certain that both genders have this lesson to learn as they are learning to soar. You can't hang on to what is weighing you down, and if you don't learn to let go, you'll never soar.

A woman called me recently, sobbing over a wayward twenty-four-year-old son who had left home and was in trouble with the law. She begged me to somehow work some magic, give her some advice, whereby she could get her son out of trouble and bring him back home. I told her that he was an adult man now, and she had to let go. I could hear the shock in her voice as she responded, "You mean, just let him go to jail?" It seemed like a cruel answer to her. But from what I knew about the situation, he needed to endure the consequences of his behavior without Mom and Dad bailing him out.

I knew that letting go was the most difficult thing for her to do. It seemed to her like the wrong thing to do. She had never even considered it. In her mind, as a mother she should solve every problem her child encountered and be there to help him out. Isn't that what good mothers do?

As we talked about the "letting go" alternative, she began to calm down. "You mean," she said, "I shouldn't do anything?" I replied, "Yes. You pray like crazy and let your son know that you love him unconditionally and always will. But other than that, you let go." She kept repeating to me, "You mean, I shouldn't do anything?" It went against all her instincts, but as she began to accept the fact that she had to let go, peace began to come into her voice. She was hopefully starting to soar again.

What are you hanging on to right now? Who are you trying to manipulate so that you can tie the bow on the package? Can you let it go? If it's too big for you to carry, that burden will keep you grounded, preventing you from soaring. Remember what Jesus told us:

> "Come to me, all you who are weary and burdened, and I will give you rest. Take my yoke upon you and learn from me, for I am gentle and humble in heart, and you will find rest for your souls. For my yoke is easy and my burden is light." (Matthew 11:28–30)

IF IT'S NOT LIGHT, IT'S NOT RIGHT!

When you and I are trying to carry something that is too heavy for us to carry, when we are refusing to let go, we are actually disobeying the command of Jesus to exchange our heavy burden for His light one. Christians aren't built to carry heavy burdens. If it's not light, it's not right!

Peter put it succinctly in his first epistle: "Cast all your anxiety on him because he cares for you" (1 Peter 5:7).

I am struck by how often God has to take me back to basics. I just keep complicating my life and my relationship with God, when it really is quite simple. Not always easy, but always simple. Just cast that heavy burden on Him. It's not yours to carry; it is His. And how do you do that? You do it by faith, by a choice to relinquish the burden, by prayer, and then trusting in the God who has promised to carry our burdens for us.

I want to share a wonderful principle with you that my friend Jill Briscoe gave me. At a point when she was trying to carry a very heavy personal burden, God showed her what she was to do. And He spoke from the story of the children of Israel bringing down the walls of Jericho.

In Joshua 6 we read this remarkable story where the Lord said to Joshua,

> "See, I have delivered Jericho into your hands. . . . March around the city once with all the armed men. Do this for six days. . . . On the seventh day, march around the city seven times. . . . When you hear them sound a long blast on the trumpets, have all the people give a loud shout; then the wall of the city will collapse and the people will go up, every man straight in."
>
> . . . So [Joshua] had the ark of the Lord carried around the city, circling it once. Then the people returned to camp and spent the night there. (Joshua 6:2b–5, 11)

Here was a problem facing God's people, and it looked like a total impossibility. How would this group of Israelites destroy the walls of Jericho and conquer the land God had promised them? Well, God gave them the directions: March around the walls with the ark of the Lord once each day. Then go back to the camp and do what you have to do that day.

Here's the principle for each of us: When you've got a burden that is heavy for you to carry and your heart is breaking and you don't know what to do, you need to march around your burden—your problem, your walls of Jericho—once each day with the ark of the Lord, the Word of God. Every morning march around that problem and tell God everything that's on your heart. Take the Word of God and find promises and comfort for yourself for the day and mentally march around that problem with the Word that God has given you.

Then, once you've marched around it once, go out and do whatever it is you must do for that day and let the burden go. Go out to soar. When the problem crops up in your mind, say, "No, sorry, but I marched around you once this morning and that's all for today. One time per day and I've left it with the Lord. It's His problem for the rest of the day."

I don't know how many days you'll have to march around your problem before those walls come down, but I do know that God has a future plan for you that is good, and that you can trust Him.

Remember, Jesus never intended for us to carry heavy burdens. When you try to carry them all day long, you can't think of anything else, you can't get anything else done, and you're no good to anyone else. The burden you're carrying starts to have drastic effects in other areas of your life, which eventually increases the burden you are carrying. You can no longer soar. It's a lose-lose situation. But if you will follow the Jericho principle and turn the heavy burden over to the Lord once a day, releasing it to Him for the rest of the day, you'll discover freedom from that impossible burden you've been trying to carry.

Of course, your enemy the devil is going to try to make you feel guilty for not carrying the burden all day long. Be prepared to stand up to the enemy and resist his attempts to dump the burden back into your hands all throughout the day. Each time you start to pick up the heavy burden, stop and pray and once again remind yourself that you were never intended to carry heavy burdens.

As wonderful as the eagle is, as majestic and brilliant and beautiful and powerful as he is as the king of birds, if he doesn't learn to let go of burdens that are too heavy, he will never soar. The same is true for us.

Remember this, "If it's not light, it's not right!" That's how you know whether or not you're carrying the right burden. *Jesus'* burden is light. You can handle it. *Your* burdens are heavy and unmanageable. Learn to let go of the heavy burdens. God never intended that you should carry them.

C H A P T E R   2

EAGLE
EYES

For my first forty years, I shamelessly bragged about my eyesight. I could see anything and everything. Signs at a great distance were crystal clear to my eyes. No print was too small for me. I showed off my superior eyesight every chance I had, boasting that I had never worn glasses or contact lenses.

Somewhere in my early forties, print began to shrink. Letters on signs were in more delicate fonts and smaller sizes. Almost overnight there seemed to be a conspiracy to take away my good eyesight—a "gotcha" for having bragged so much.

First came reading glasses for close work, such as computers and reading. Then I added contacts to my repertoire so that I could read my notes when speaking. Now I'm dependent on them, and I often long for the days when I could see anything without a problem. Every time I lose my glasses, every time I have to dig them out of my purse in order to see a price tag in a store, every time I'm straining to read that sign up ahead, I long for the exceptional eyesight that was mine for so long.

But as important as physical eyesight is, spiritual eyesight is even more so. Jesus said: "The eye is the lamp of the body. If your eyes are good, your whole body will be full of light. But if your eyes are bad, your whole body will be full of darkness. If then the light within you is darkness, how great is that darkness!" (Matthew 6:22–23).

Jesus was speaking of spiritual eyes and spiritual darkness. Physical blindness is a regrettable condition, and we have compassion toward those who must live in this world without their physical eyesight. But sadder by far is the Christian who lives without spiritual eyesight.

EAGLES HAVE REMARKABLE EYESIGHT

We've all heard the expression "He's got an eagle eye." And we recognize that to mean that a person has the ability to see things well; he doesn't miss a thing. The expression comes from the fact that the eagle's eyesight is legendary. It is four to eight times stronger than human eyesight.

The eagle's eyes are so large they occupy most of the area in the skull. In addition to the power of the eagle's unusual eyes, its vision is binocular, which gives an eagle the ability to alter his focus from two feet to two miles. It's as though the eagle's eyes are like the zoom lens of a powerful camera or binoculars, and he is able to adjust his focus to see not only what is close up, but also what is at a great distance.

In addition, the eagle has a second eyelid, as it were. These are ridges that overhang the eyes and help protect them from injury when the eagle is catching and handling its prey. This second eyelid also shields the eagle from the sun, acting like sunglasses and greatly reducing the glare. This allows an eagle to fly right into the sun without being blinded by it.

The eagle's eyesight gives him a great advantage over other birds. He sees things coming and can be prepared. From long distances he spots trouble and can avoid it. He sees a potential meal a long way off and is able to find his food easier than other birds can. With that powerful eyesight, he is not easily fooled or surprised.

FOREVER EYES

Christians, too, have a unique advantage when it comes to eyesight. We can see the unseen. The apostle Paul wrote: "So we fix our eyes not on what is seen, but on what is unseen. For what is seen is temporary, but what is unseen is eternal" (2 Corinthians 4:18).

Since we're all rational, practical people, we might ask the apostle, "How in the world can anyone see what is unseen? Those are contradictory terms. If it is unseen, then by definition it cannot be seen—right?"

Well, not exactly. It's true, not many people can see what is unseen, but when you have Forever Eyes, you can. Forever Eyes are God's eyes, and as Christians, born from above, we can see through God's eyes.

Colossians 1:16 tells us: "For by him [Jesus] all things were created: things in heaven and on earth, visible and invisible, whether thrones or powers or rulers or authorities; all things were created by him and for him."

These invisible things which can be seen through Forever Eyes are not some mystical, magical vapors. They are not figments of our imagination. We're not talking about visualizing things that are *not* there, but rather about seeing things that are there. They are real things, created by Jesus, just as real as the visible things our natural eyes can behold.

We tend to think of the visible world as real and doubt the reality of any other. Our five senses clamor upon us and demand to be accepted as real and final. Sin has so clouded the lens of our hearts that we cannot see the other reality shining around us. But this invisible world is not the future. It is now.

What are some of the unseen things we can see through Forever Eyes? Paul clearly tells us in 2 Corinthians 4:18 that the things which are unseen are the things that are eternal; that is, they are the things which will endure forever and have eternal significance. In contrast, the visible things are the temporary things that will not endure forever.

Consider these real but invisible things:

- God is invisible. Yet Scripture says, "Taste and see the Lord is good" (Psalm 34:8). "My sheep hear My voice" (John 10:27 NASB). "Blessed are the pure in heart, for they will see God" (Matthew 5:8). The Holy Spirit uses *taste, hear,* and *see* to help us understand that God, though invisible to earthly eyes, can be seen with Forever Eyes.
- Faith, hope, and love are invisible. Yet we know that when all the visible things are gone, these will still be there. "And

now these three remain: faith, hope and love. But the greatest of these is love" (1 Corinthians 13:13). With Forever Eyes, you can see the importance and the impact of faith, hope, and love and the incredible power that is ours because we are given the ability to have faith, hope, and love.

- The souls of people are invisible. Yet these will endure forever. And with Forever Eyes, we can look beyond the external façade of the people around us and see their eternal souls.

FIXING OUR EYES

Paul says we have to *fix* our eyes on what is unseen: "So we fix our eyes not on what is seen, but on what is unseen. For what is seen is temporary, but what is unseen is eternal" (2 Corinthians 4:18).

If we don't do that, we'll miss the unseen and see only what can be seen. And when we don't see what is unseen, we lose our Christian perspective and view everything the same way everyone else does. In other words, we are given these extraordinary eagle eyes, these Forever Eyes, but we can choose not to use them.

What does it mean to fix our eyes on what is unseen? It means a volitional act of our will. We do it on purpose; we do it decidedly; we do it by looking all the time—continual staring, if you please! It takes effort; it takes awareness; it takes reminders; it takes discipline. We pray it into our lives.

Don't worry about being so "heavenly minded that you're no earthly good." It has never happened! Being heavenly minded means your mind thinks about the things of God, your eyes see things the way God does. Fixing your eyes on the unseen things is heavenly mindedness.

WHAT DO PEOPLE
LOOK LIKE THROUGH FOREVER EYES?

Who is the most difficult person in your life right now? Have you ever looked at her or him through Forever Eyes? It may be a co-worker who has poor work habits or an offensive personality. It could be a family member who has never affirmed you or, worse yet, has abused you. It could be a person at your church who seems intent on making your life miserable.

Ever notice how often this person can ruin your day? That's because you are seeing the "seen" things about that person—the things that everyone else sees. I would challenge you to put on Forever Eyes and ask God to help you see this person the way He does.

I well remember a very difficult man for whom I used to work. I allowed him to upset me almost every workday for a year. Finally I stopped asking God to give me a new job and began asking what He wanted me to learn. That's when I finally put on my Forever Eyes and saw this man in an entirely different light. I saw his miserableness; I understood his lack of confidence; I felt sorry for him because he didn't have Jesus in his life.

Forever Eyes allow you to see a person's eternal soul, to realize that God loves him and died for him, and to start focusing on what is really important—that person's eternal destiny. Forever Eyes allow you to see a broken heart, a tragic past, an insecurity, a lack of confidence.

The next two years working for this man were drastically changed when I began putting on Forever Eyes. He didn't change dramatically, but I did, and that gave me the understanding and patience to stay there and actually have compassion for this man. By the way, Forever Eyes also reduced my stress, made a much better worker out of me, and greatly improved my witness on the job.

WHAT DO MONEY AND SUCCESS LOOK LIKE THROUGH FOREVER EYES?

Without Forever Eyes we can easily become addicted to and obsessed by money and what we think it can do for us. It's just as easy for a Christian to get caught up in this money-success madness as it is anyone else.

When I came back to God and began my radio ministry over sixteen years ago, a very successful man whom I had known during the years of "doing my own thing" came into town and we had dinner together. I thought he would be impressed with my commitment to the Lord and to this new ministry, but not so. He couldn't believe that I was pursuing this endeavor, which would not pay me any money or advance my career. In his words, "I thought you were smarter than that, Mary."

The difference was that he was the slave of money; it represented success to him. He was looking at the visible things. God had given me new eyesight. Looking through Forever Eyes, I was thrilled to be used by God in this new ministry and saw success as doing what God had called me to do.

I must confess that it is still easy for me to see money and success the way the world does, and there have been times when I've again looked through earthly eyes. Inevitably when I do, I inflict a great deal of unnecessary worry on myself and allow myself to be in bondage again to money.

As soon as I put on Forever Eyes, I remember that God has promised to provide for all my needs if I seek first His Kingdom and His righteousness (Matthew 6:33). I relearn the truth that my success in eternity's viewpoint will have nothing to do with my financial status here on earth. And then the worry and care subside, and I am again resting in His care.

WHAT DO POSSESSIONS LOOK LIKE THROUGH FOREVER EYES?

I remember when some years ago our church suffered a terrible fire caused by an arsonist. Our beautiful concert grand piano, pipe organ, and carved pulpit went up in smoke, and there was a great deal of other damage. I stood in the church that day, viewing the ruins with tears pouring down my face at the loss we had suffered. But in that moment God spoke to me with a message I've never forgotten. The Spirit of God quietly said, "They were going to burn up anyway," and I was reminded that all the earthly things we treasure will not last for eternity. They will all burn up someday.

Do you possess your possessions, or do they possess you? Once you learn to look at what you own through Forever Eyes, you are going to know a freedom you won't believe. You may have no idea just how much stress and worry you add to your life through the accumulation of things—stuff! It's not that owning things is wrong, but when they become the "apples of our eyes," we lose that eternal perspective.

For some people, the only way to avoid being possessed by possessions is to get rid of them. For others, it is to adopt a continual change of attitude toward them. Anything like this ever happen to you?

- A neighbor asks to borrow your car because hers is in the shop for repairs. She just needs to run a few errands. You agree. Two hours later your phone rings; she's had an accident. Nobody's hurt, but your car is pretty banged up.
- Your father wants to help you pack and move. He is wrapping your good, expensive china, and, without meaning to, drops the vegetable bowl and it breaks into pieces.
- Your daughter has a few friends over for a slumber party. They're nice girls, but normal. One of them gets chocolate ice cream on your new sofa.

Cars and china and sofas—they are the visible things that are easy to see and touch and feel. But they are temporary. When you put on your Forever Eyes, you see the invisible things. You see the soul of that neighbor who needs to know Jesus, and you realize that how you react to the car damage will make an impression on her. You see the eyes of your father and how bad he feels, and easing his guilt feelings is more important than a broken bowl. You see your daughter's look of fear as she wonders what you're going to say to her friend, and you decide that trust and relationship with your daughter are far more important than a stain on the sofa.

Those Forever Eyes give you an entirely different view of material things. You realize that they're all going to burn up someday. Only what you send on ahead of yourself will endure.

WHAT DO YOUR CIRCUMSTANCES LOOK LIKE THROUGH FOREVER EYES?

Undoubtedly everything in your life is not just the way you want it. You wish you were married, you wish you had married someone else, you wish your children were different, you wish you had children—the list is endless. But when you look at the missing things in your life through Forever Eyes, it gives you a very different view.

Ask yourself, how many more years do you think you will live, if you live to be very old? It could be thirty or forty or fifty or seventy—pick a number. Then compare that number to eternity. This world is not the most important part of our lives; eternity is far more important. With Forever Eyes you can look at your circumstances and say, "Well, it would be nice to—whatever, fill in the blank—but I have only a few years here, and then in eternity I will be complete, lacking nothing."

When you put on Forever Eyes, the temporary circumstances of your life that may be difficult or miserable or unfair or painful will not seem nearly so important. You will be far more content and far less focused on what you don't have when you wear Forever Eyes.

FOREVER EYES BRING CHANGES

Let me warn you, as I do myself, that Forever Eyes will undoubtedly cause some significant changes in your life. Forever Eyes change your life's priorities. Forever Eyes are focused on other people, not on yourself. Forever Eyes require a level of commitment far beyond what most Christians are accustomed to giving.

Someone wrote: *I refuse to let what will rot rule the eternal.*

That's a very good sentence to tuck away in the back of your mind. Compare what is going to rot with what is eternal:

What Will Rot?	**What Is Eternal?**
• My physical body	• My spirit
• My job	• My calling
• My things	• People's souls
• Television	• God's Word
• My accomplishments	• Servanthood
• My money	• Treasures in heaven
• My problems	• Joy, peace, hope, faith, love

Jim Elliot's famous line is familiar to most Christians: "He is no fool who gives up what he cannot keep to gain what he cannot lose."[1] Have you been paying more attention to the things that will rot than the things that are eternal? You need to learn the great freedom and joy of wearing eagle's eyes—those Forever Eyes!

FOREVER EYES REAP GREAT BENEFITS HERE AND IN ETERNITY

Second Corinthians 4:16–17 reminds us of what happens when we have an eternal viewpoint and see the unseen things: "Therefore we do not lose heart. Though outwardly we are wasting away, yet inwardly we are being renewed day by day. For our light and momentary troubles are achieving for us an eternal glory that far outweighs them all."

The glory that awaits those of us who look through Forever Eyes far outweighs anything we can imagine in this temporal world. Forever Eyes renew us on the inside day by day; they are like a spring of water bubbling up inside of us, keeping us going. Therefore, the apostle Paul said, "we do not lose heart."

Years ago I began asking God to give me Forever Eyes to help me for the day ahead to see things the way He sees them, to enable me to view everything that comes my way—small and large—through His perspective. I know I have to consciously fix my eyes on the unseen things because the visible things are very alluring. It's much easier to see the visible things, but it's much more wonderful to see the invisible things.

USE YOUR EAGLE EYES

The eagle has been given the power to see what other birds cannot. Similarly, because of our spiritual insight, we have been given the marvelous ability to see what other persons cannot. Like the eagle's eye that guards and protects that proud bird, so our Forever Eyes can help us avoid dangers ahead and keep us from stumbling. Like the eagle, who can fly into the sun because of the unique design of his eyes, so we can fly right to the Son, Jesus Christ. There we will find protection from our enemies, strength to help in our times of need, and an eternal perspective of everything and everyone in our world.

Don't forget to use your eagle's eyes—your Forever Eyes. They are a wonderful advantage we have because of Jesus.

EAGLE
FLYING
LESSONS

In my younger days, I decided that I wanted to ski. I watched skiers on television and it didn't look too difficult. I had friends who could ski, so why couldn't I? So, with rented skis and borrowed ski clothes, I headed up to a ski resort in New England with a few friends, eagerly looking forward to this marvelous experience of skiing.

As we made our way to the slopes, I looked up at what seemed a fairly small hill; I watched others floating down it effortlessly, and I decided there was nothing to fear. So, with no lessons, no training, not even a few tips from friends, I took the ski lift up to the top of that hill.

But what I couldn't see from the bottom was the steep pitch you had to maneuver as you got off the lift. As the lift paused for me to disembark, I clung to the seat frozen in fear. The operator kept motioning for me to get off; I looked at him in disbelief. Nobody had taught me how to disembark.

Somehow, after holding up the lift for a considerable time, I awkwardly and ungracefully fell out. Well, you would think that would have been a warning sign to me, but I figured that the worst part was behind me, and now I went to tackle the hill. Mind you, I didn't even know how to snowplow or stop. As I shuffled around to the hilltop, my heart stopped beating. Below me was this incredibly steep and long incline, which was far different from the view at the bottom. People were passing around me, headed down the hill, but fear set in such as I've seldom known. My impulse was to somehow get back on that lift and go back down, but they don't allow you to do that.

As I was standing there, considering my plight, the wind, which was very strong that day, caught me from behind and I started down the hill, propelled by the wind and totally out of control but momentarily appearing to be skiing skillfully. One of my ski-experienced friends happened to fly by me at that moment, and was impressed to see me maneuvering so well. "Good job," he yelled, never realizing that I was a disaster looking for a place to happen!

The disaster did happen about one-quarter of the way down the hill, as my skis went one way and I another, landing on my back in a bank of snow. Finally a couple of experienced friends came by, recognized my dilemma, collected my skis for me, and gingerly helped me snowplow down the hill. Then I was directed to the beginner's hill, given some basic beginner's instructions, and I began to learn how to ski—along with the five- and six-year-olds!

Skiing did not come naturally for me. I needed lessons and training. Just having skis and the necessary clothes and equipment did not mean I could begin skiing right off the bat. I had to learn how to ski.

An eaglet has to learn how to soar. Even though she has wings, she needs flying lessons. Let's look at how a baby eagle learns to soar.

A COZY NEST

Mama eagle will lay one to three eggs annually in the springtime. Once the female eagle lays her eggs, she or her mate must stay with them, keeping them warm during incubation. Interestingly, that responsibility is shared by both parents, as are hunting, nest watching, and eagle brooding.

As the time approaches for the eggs to hatch, the mother eagle will begin to pull from her breast a downy fur to prepare a soft, warm bedding for her babies. Both parents are very devoted to their offspring, and they make the nest as comfortable and safe as possible for their precious eaglets to be born. And there in the warm, soft, safe place, the eaglets are born and happily spend their first days and weeks there.

Soon after baby eagle is born, she begins a cry that will last for several weeks. It is a constant cry for food, and Mama and Papa eagle stay busy from morning 'til night trying to round up enough food for the hungry babies.

So the baby eagle settles into her new home, never realizing that this is not her permanent abode. Never even knowing she has wings to fly and soar. While baby eagle is safely tucked in the nest, getting stronger and growing bigger every day, Mama and Papa soar and hover over her, showing her what eagles are meant to do. But with such a comfortable nest, baby eagle is content to be a freeloader and just let Mom and Dad take care of her.

Each day, as the eaglet gets bigger, her wings become stronger. But she doesn't pay attention. Life is wonderful when you're a baby. People pet you and carry you and make over you and put up with your fits. You don't have to worry about paying the bills or buying groceries or getting along with people. Everybody has to get along with you, and when you need help, they're there to help you. Why should a baby eaglet leave the nest when life is so good?

AN UNFEATHERED NEST

But one day, when the baby eagle is about three months old and about 80 percent of its full-grown size, Mama and Papa start behaving very strangely. Mama stomps into the nest, squawking and throwing all the soft fur and feathers out and sweeping the nest with her great wings. With all the softness gone, the nest becomes uncomfortable, with scratchy sticks and branches coming from every direction. No longer is it a cushiony place for baby eagle to lie around and relax. The eaglet must now stand on her own two talons to avoid the unpleasant abrasiveness of the nest.

This causes her to learn to balance herself, and her talons grow stronger because she has to stand all day. So Mama and Papa eagle have a good reason for putting the baby through this uncomfortable stage, but the eaglet does not understand what is happening. All baby knows is that life used to be comfortable and she felt very protected and loved by her parents, and now it seems as though those same parents are causing her misery and making her life dreary on purpose. But Mama and Papa eagle are willing to be misunderstood by their own child in order to help her grow into the mature eagle she is meant to be.

THE MATURITY BROUGHT
BY COMFORT REMOVAL

Did you know that God is more concerned with your maturity than with your comfort? And it seems that for all of us, our growth into a mature Christian comes most often by "comfort removal" in our lives. God is willing to be misunderstood by you, if necessary, rather than allow you to settle for immaturity and never realize your potential.

James wrote: "Consider it pure joy, my brothers, whenever you face trials of many kinds, because you know that the testing of your faith develops perseverance. Perseverance must finish its work so that you may be mature and complete, not lacking anything" (James 1:2–4).

Consider it pure joy? Does that sound unrealistic to you? Consider that word *consider*. It has the meaning of "think forward." So, we might paraphrase it like this:

Think forward whenever you find yourself in uncomfortable situations that you don't understand. Think of the end result and realize that this trial you're facing can help you develop into the mature Christian you really want to be. It will help you to become complete in your faith, having everything you need to live a godly life and bring glory to the Lord.

God doesn't expect us to throw a party when times are tough, when the feathers have been taken from our nests and life is very uncomfortable. That would be a phony joy. But we can learn to "think forward" beyond the difficulties of the moment and consider the good that is going to come from the difficult experience. It is a matter of choosing what you will think about—the present difficulties or the future good.

The writer to the Hebrews understood this. He wrote, "No discipline seems pleasant at the time, but painful. Later on, however, it produces a harvest of righteousness and peace for those who have been trained by it" (Hebrews 12:11).

That's what we have to learn to think about when our nests are suddenly de-comforted and life has no more smooth places in which to rest.

A friend was recently telling me about some very difficult circumstances in her life, having to do with her medical practice. She is a physician and had made very good plans for enlarging her practice in order to help more people. But through no fault of her own, a man she trusted turned out to be a thief and she lost most of the money and assets she had worked so long and hard to accumulate. It was a devastating situation from an earthly perspective.

But throughout her entire recitation, she continually reaffirmed that she knew that God was going to work this out for her good and that she was trusting Him in the midst of the panic and loss to turn this into His glory. She was thinking forward; she was enduring the pain of the present in anticipation of the harvest of righteousness that would come as a result. She was submitting to the training that comes through discipline, painful though it may be.

In our twenty-first-century culture, we are programmed for speed and instant gratification. Thinking forward is not a skill we easily learn. Enduring present pain for future glory is foreign to our mental processes. What often happens is that as we go through the difficult, painful circumstances and are subjected to the prickly nest that has lost its soft covering, we never realize the benefits that can come from it.

Paul wrote to the Galatians, "Have you suffered so much for nothing—if it really was for nothing?" (Galatians 3:4). Suffering for nothing—never realizing the benefits that are ours when we accept suffering—is the lot for many people. They endure the hardship but never enjoy the benefit. They waste their suffering.

If you're not in a difficult circumstance at this point in your life, you will likely encounter one before too long. If soft feathers are lining your nest and making life comfortable right now, enjoy them, but understand that there will come a day when suddenly your nest no longer is comfortable.

On the other hand, if you're in that predicament of wondering what is happening, what God is up to, and why He has taken all the feathers from your nest, are you wasting your sorrows? Can you think forward and see the good that will come, provided you are willing to be trained by your trial?

A baby eagle has no ability to think forward; she has no capacity to understand the good that is going to come when Mama eagle starts taking the comfort away. But if you're a child of God, you have the presence and the power of God's Holy Spirit resident in your body, enabling you to think with the mind of Christ and see beyond your present troubles. Therefore, turn the difficulties into a training session for your future benefit and God's glory.

Elisabeth Elliot wrote:

> God has allowed in the lives of each of us some sort of loss, the withdrawal of something we valued, in order that we may learn to offer ourselves a little more willingly, to allow the touch of death on one more thing we have clutched so tightly, and thus know fullness and freedom and joy that much sooner. We're not naturally inclined to love God and seek His Kingdom. Trouble may help to incline us—that is, it may tip us over, put some pressure on us, lean us in the right direction.[1]

PUSHED OUT OF THE NEST

As if the comfort removal were not enough, Mama eagle then proceeds to do what seems even more cruel. She jumps into the nest and starts fluttering her huge wings. This frightens the eaglet and she screams, but Papa doesn't intervene to stop Mama. He just circles over the nest, keeping his eye on everything that is happening. He never takes his eyes off the baby eagle.

Mama eagle begins pushing that baby eagle with her wings, grabbing it with her huge talons—as big as a man's hand—until she maneuvers that baby to the edge of the nest. Baby eagle looks over the edge, perched in the heights as it is, and sees total disaster. Having no understanding of what Mama eagle is up to, and fearing the danger that lurks on the rocks below, baby eagle screams for help as she sits on the nest edge.

Then suddenly, without warning, Mama eagle pushes the baby over the edge. This begins a free fall toward the rocks below, and baby eagle feels totally helpless. She flaps her young and clumsy wings until she is so weak she can no longer flap. She is doomed to be dashed on the rocks below.

However, Papa, hovering overhead, with perfect timing, swoops down with incredible speed and rescues that baby eagle, spreading his wings underneath the baby, just before she crashes into the ground. Just in the nick of time, Papa saves the baby and returns it to the nest. You see, an eaglet cannot fall faster than her father can fly.

This pattern is repeated as many times as is necessary until the baby eagle realizes that by spreading her wings and catching the wind current, she can soar like Mama and Papa. This is a completely new experience for baby eagle, and she now recognizes that she was born to soar. She loves soaring. How much better this is than sitting in a nest and squawking all day long. With wings outstretched, she has freedom to enjoy the beauty of her surroundings, to find her own meal, to express her own creativity, to do what she was born to do—soar!

Now, with twenty-twenty hindsight, she understands that her parents were training her for flight. What seemed cruel has turned out for her good.

Mama and Papa eagle celebrate their child's achievement by locking talons and doing acrobatics in the air. They endured their little one's anger and protests and fear so that this baby could grow to maturity and soar like an eagle.

LEARNING HOW TO SOAR

The analogies here between the eagle and our own experience as Christians make clear why the eagle is used in Scripture as an illustration for us. When we're born from above, we are given a new nature—our "eagle nature," if you will. But even though we're born with wings to soar, we have to take soaring lessons.

No doubt you've had a few of those in your life as a believer. Can you remember a time when you felt you had been pushed over the edge, you had no idea what God was doing in your life, and you were angry and frightened and disillusioned with it all? Maybe that's where you are right now.

I want to reassure you that your heavenly Father has not forgotten you. He never takes His eyes off of you.

But the eyes of the Lord are on those who fear him,
on those whose hope is in his unfailing love.
—Psalm 33:18

The eyes of the Lord are on the righteous
and his ears are attentive to their cry.
—*Psalm 34:15*

If you've been crying some lately, figuratively or actually, God has heard your cries; He has seen your tears. He is touched with the feelings of your infirmities and is not oblivious to your fear and pain. Though you have not felt His presence or seen evidence of His involvement, be assured that He has been with you all the way.

I think it is most difficult for us to believe this when the predicament we are in is not our fault, and is indeed caused by sin on the part of someone else. How can this be a soaring lesson? Why would God allow this to happen to us? Surely He would not impose this evil in our lives just to teach us to trust Him. There must be a better way to learn to soar.

Why *do* bad things happen to good people? How can a good God permit evil in the lives of His children? These questions have haunted the Christian family since its beginning, and people far more qualified and learned than I am have written book after book to try to help us come to grips with these troubling issues. It is helpful to read these good books, but at the end of the day, there are still unanswered questions that the most theologically brilliant person cannot resolve to our satisfaction.

We know that God is not the author of evil, but He allows evil in this world for a season. Evil and sin are at the heart of many of our difficult circumstances, and we understand that sin has spoiled God's creation and corrupted our society. Nonetheless, we still wonder why our soaring lessons are so often a result of the sin and evil of another person.

BACK TO THE BASICS

In our finite thinking we must finally rest on some solid rocks of our faith.

- God is above and beyond us and we will never fully understand His ways this side of heaven. The psalmist said: "Our God is in heaven; he does whatever pleases him" (Psalm 115:3).

Isaiah asked, "Who has understood the mind of the LORD, or instructed him as his counselor?" (Isaiah 40:13). "'My thoughts are not your thoughts, neither are your ways my ways,' declares the LORD" (Isaiah 55:8).

- God's ways are holy and right, even when we don't understand them. The psalmist proclaimed: "Your ways, O God, are holy. What god is so great as our God?" (Psalm 77:13). At the end of his life, Moses asserted: "I will proclaim the name of the LORD. Oh, praise the greatness of our God! He is the Rock, his works are perfect, and all his ways are just. A faithful God who does no wrong, upright and just is he" (Deuteronomy 32:3–4).

- God is trustworthy, even when we can't see the path in front of us. We have the sure promise of God: "'For I know the plans I have for you,' declares the LORD, 'plans to prosper you and not to harm you, plans to give you hope and a future'" (Jeremiah 29:11).

Soaring lessons are rarely pleasant. Given our way, we would never leave our comfortable nests, would we? If we were to choose our own path we would never consciously include a free fall to the rocks below. But even in the midst of that free fall, we can rely on a heavenly Father who never takes His eyes off us and whose ear is attentive to our every cry.

OUR PROMISE OF PROTECTION

Furthermore, and most importantly, you can be assured that the Lord God will not allow you to be dashed on the rocks below because, like the eagle, your heavenly Father can fly faster than you can fall.

In the Song of Moses, Moses reminded the whole assembly of Israel that the Lord their God had shielded them, cared for them, and guarded them as the apple of His eye. He said that God had been to them "like an eagle that stirs up its nest and hovers over its young, that spreads its wings to catch them and carries them on its pinions" (Deuteronomy 32:11).

David, the man after God's own heart, was pushed out of his nest in some seemingly cruel ways as Saul pursued him relentlessly, trying to kill him. But it was during these difficult times that David learned to soar and came to realize that his heavenly Father had never forsaken him. He wrote: "[The LORD] reached down from on high and took hold of me; he drew me out of deep waters. . . . he rescued me because he delighted in me" (Psalm 18:16, 19b).

In the glorious 91st Psalm, we are told: "For he [the Most High] will command his angels concerning you to guard you in all your ways; they will lift you up in their hands, so that you will not strike your foot against a stone" (Psalm 91:11–12).

A well-known benediction given to us by Jude reminds us again of God's constant care: "To him who is able to keep you from falling and to present you before his glorious presence without fault and with great joy . . ." (Jude 24).

A PERSONAL GOD

The God of Moses and David and Jude is still God today, and He is our God—not only a God of all power and wisdom and strength, but a personal God who is intimately interested in each one of us. That never ceases to amaze me—that the God of all the universe should bother to care about me. It's one of the truths about God that blows a circuit in the human mind and is beyond our ability to register. It must be accepted in simple childlike faith and then enjoyed to the hilt!

Just to think that God Himself is willing to give us soaring lessons. To take the time and care and attention necessary for us earthbound types to learn to soar like eagles. What an exciting prospect, even though the soaring lessons are never easy and sometimes very confusing. How wonderful to know that our God, the true and only God, never takes His eyes off us and, indeed, is totally capable of flying faster than we can fall. Like the children of Israel, He hovers over us and spreads His wings to catch us, carrying us on His pinions—His wings.

If you take nothing else from this book, take this picture with you and never forget it. The God of eternity, the great I AM, Jehovah God, the First and the Last, the Creator of heaven and earth—this same God is watching you and ready to spread His wings so that you will never be dashed against the rocks. He is hovering over you—waiting near at hand, lingering all around you. And you can rest assured that He will be there to spread His wings and catch you, because you cannot fall faster than He can fly.

THE JOYS OF SOARING

Once you get the gist of soaring, you won't ever settle for anything else. Maybe you're wondering what it means for us to soar like an eagle. It doesn't mean that life is easy and pain-free. It doesn't mean there are no more wrinkles to encounter, because in soaring you will encounter winds and storms and adversities in the sky.

The joy of soaring comes in having a victorious lifestyle, where you are not defeated by the adversities. The joy of soaring is in the closeness you find in those high places with God. The joy of soaring is knowing that your heavenly Father is pleased to watch you soar, is rejoicing over you, just as the parent eagles rejoice over their young eagle.

Think of this: "The LORD your God is with you, he is mighty to save. He will take great delight in you, he will quiet you with his love, he will rejoice over you with singing" (Zephaniah 3:17).

Can you envision the Lord your God rejoicing over you with singing? We rejoice over God with our songs of praise, but to think that He rejoices over us with singing and takes great delight in us! What joy! What incredible joy! Think of the parent eagles clasping talons and performing a dance of joy in the sky when their little one spreads his wings and soars. And then think of your heavenly Father rejoicing over you. Nothing else truly compares to that kind of eternal and internal joy.

THE EAGLE'S
FLYING
SECRET

Samson must have been some guy. In today's jargon he would be described as a hunk; a ladies' man; a heartthrob. As a Nazirite he was set apart to God from birth, and his purpose in life was to deliver Israel from the hands of the Philistines. His acts of bravery and exceptional strength are legendary, from tearing a lion apart with his bare hands, to catching three hundred foxes and turning them into living torches, to single-handedly killing a thousand men with the jawbone of a donkey. (See chapters 13 through 16 of Judges.)

There was a secret to Samson's power: his unshaved head. His covenant with God was that his head would never be shaved, and if it were, he would become as weak as any other man. Samson knew this, and for many years he kept his head unshaved in obedience to God and in recognition of the true source of his power.

But one fatal day he was tricked into revealing his secret by the delightfully deceptive Delilah—and you know the rest of the story. She shaved his head, and that was the end of his reign over Israel. In his own power Samson was helpless.

This is a lifelong lesson for all of us. It seems as though I have to reenter the school of learning to trust and take that Trusting 101 course time and again, for as soon as I take my eyes off of Jesus, I start thinking that I can succeed in my own power—and then I discover how weak I truly am.

Eagles have a similar lesson to learn. With all of their strength and speed and majesty and ability, if they try to fly by flapping, it will be disastrous.

FLAPPING EAGLES CAN'T SOAR

With their unique wing structure, eagles can soar effortlessly for hours because they allow wind currents and thermal updrafts to carry them. But when they try to flap those huge wings, their strength is quickly dissipated and they cannot sustain flight for long. In fact, a flapping eagle will eventually become so exhausted he would die if he were not able to catch the wind current and go from flapping to soaring.

This is a major lesson for an eagle to learn as he begins life on his own. Catch the wind current, and you will soar like an eagle. Try to flap your way through the skies, and you will soon be exhausted, perhaps even dead.

OUR PERFORMANCE-DRIVEN LIVES

From our earliest years we learn that our performance determines whether we have or have not; whether we win or lose; whether we succeed or fail. Before babies can talk we're telling them they're good boys or good girls, or bad boys or bad girls, based on their performance. If they obey and behave well, they're good; if they pitch a temper tantrum and disobey, they're bad.

Once we start to school, we learn that our performance determines our grade. Our grades determine whether we get promoted or not. Our school record determines what college we can go to. We have to perform in order to achieve academic success.

We start our careers and discover quickly that this performance-driven philosophy carries over to our jobs. When I was in IBM sales, the one criterion for success was "How much did you sell?" When I sold a lot and exceeded my quota, I was rewarded with money, recognition, and eventually a promotion. When I didn't, I hung my head and tried to avoid my manager, because my performance was not up to expectations.

Even with our parents and family, we can find that love is given or withheld based on performance. This should not be true, but it happens. I hear from many people who even as adults are still injured because they couldn't perform to their parents' expectations and so lost their approval and sometimes love because of poor performance.

It happens with mates as well. People get married and then find that their mate has performance expectations. When they don't or can't live up to those expectations, love and devotion and loyalty are withheld and the marriage often breaks up because it was based on performance.

Many people think they have to perform in order to earn love and care.

LIVING IN LEGALISM AND GUILT

To live in a performance-driven world is to live in legalism. Certain standards or expectations—or laws—are placed upon us, and we strive to abide and achieve. When we succeed, we feel good about ourselves; we are very proud of ourselves. When we fail, we get down on ourselves and live in guilt.

Living in a performance-driven world leads us to lots of comparing. If my performance is better than yours, I feel better than you. If I am better than lots of other people at something, I really feel good about myself and think I'm something special. If, on the other hand, you out-perform me, I'm in trouble, because I base my worth on how I perform compared to you or someone else.

Because we all live in a performance-driven world, this thinking gets into our psyche and can do us great damage when it comes to our relationship with God. The most difficult thing for most people to understand and accept in coming to God is that they can never impress Him with their performance. Nor can they ever perform up to His standards. Therefore, they cannot earn anything from God.

Paul wrote to the Romans: "Therefore no one will be declared righteous in [God's] sight by observing the law; rather, through the law we become conscious of sin" (Romans 3:20).

If you know anything about the Bible, you know that the Old Testament is full of the Law God gave to Moses and his people. The Israelites were taught to live by a very strict law, which told them exactly how to perform. When they lived by the Law and obeyed God, they prospered. When they failed to do that, they found themselves in all kinds of trouble.

My reading in the Old Testament has me now in Leviticus. I never enjoy studying Leviticus. It is just one legal requirement after another. I get tired and depressed just reading about all the sacrifices that had to be offered in exactly the right way. But that book is in the Bible for a purpose—to show us what it's like to live under law.

The first seven chapters of Leviticus give all the regulations for the different offerings: the burnt offering, the grain offering, the sin offering, the guilt offering, the ordination offering, and the fellowship offering. And they had to be offered in exactly the right way.

As I was reading those chapters, it began to dawn on me why God wants me to read Leviticus every once in a while. I need to know what living under the Law is like. It is burdensome; it is impossible. And it is totally performance driven. The one word that pops out at you all through that book is *guilt!* It has to do with being guilty, breaking the Law, and making a sacrificial offering to God to make up for your bad performance.

We know that the children of Israel miserably failed, for the most part, to live up to God's Law. They could not keep the Law, and therefore they could not earn a relationship with God through performance. However, if you read Leviticus, I think you'll agree that we would have failed, too.

THE PURPOSE OF THE LAW

So why did God give the Law? He had to know we couldn't live up to it. We need to understand this. God did not "try out" the Law to see if it would work and then, discovering that we were incapable of keeping the Law, come up with Plan B. No, God knew from the beginning that we could never keep the Law and thereby earn a relationship with Him through performance. The Law was given to show us how far short we will always fall in our performance, no matter how good we think we are or how hard we work.

I look at the standard—for example, "Love the Lord your God with all your heart and with all your soul and with all your strength" (Deuteronomy 6:5)—and I know immediately that I have never fully kept that law and will *never* fully do so. The Law shows me how unacceptable my performance is; without the Law to tell me that, I might think I was OK by comparing myself with others. But with the Law, I know what God's standards are, and I know I can't keep them.

GOD'S PROVISION FOR OUR FAILURE

What's the answer? Well, God knew from the beginning that we would fail to keep the Law, and He planned the solution to the problem before the foundation of the world. Our inability to perform to His standards did not take God by surprise; He knew that once sin entered into the world, we were all doomed to fail. Therefore, He sent Jesus to be the perfect sacrifice, the one Person who could earn God's favor through performance because He was and is the sinless Son of God. This One came to be our sacrifice for sin because He is perfect. And His performance on the cross and His resurrection from the dead provide for us the answer to our dilemma.

So in order to become a child of God, I must give up trying to perform up to His standards. That's what it means to be born again. I recognize my total inability to perform my way into heaven. I accept what Jesus said, that to enter the kingdom of God I must be born again, with a new heart and by His Spirit, and then I am enabled to become His child. That comes through acceptance and trust, not through performance. "He saved us, not because of righteous things we had done, but because of his mercy" (Titus 3:5).

TRYING TO PLEASE GOD THROUGH PERFORMANCE

Many of us can say, "Yes, I know I can't earn my way to heaven; going to church won't do it; taking communion won't do it; being baptized won't do it; living as good a life as I can won't do it. I must accept the free gift He offers, and because Jesus is acceptable to God, I am acceptable to God." We've crossed that threshold and finally got that through our heads and we're now children of God.

But then what happens? Well, we start to live out the Christian life and fall right back into a performance-driven mentality. Now that I'm a child of God, I'm going to perform and prove what a good Christian I am by my performance—right?

When I was a teenager, I was caught up in the legalistic mind-set of the day in evangelical circles. We had our list of things you could and couldn't do, but the list of "couldn't do" was very long—no movies, no dancing, no smoking or drinking, no bad language, no immorality. Some people went much further: no makeup, no fancy hairstyles. And we judged our spiritual status based on performance. I think we were more interested in the approval of people than we were the approval of God, and we were caught up in a performance-driven Christian life.

Romans 5:10 says: "For if, when we were God's enemies, we were reconciled to him through the death of his Son, how much more, having been reconciled, shall we be saved through his life!"

When Christians, who are truly born again, live a lifeless existence, it is because they don't understand who they are in Jesus. Most of them are trying their best to perform up to God's standards. Yes, they accepted Christ by faith and believe they'll get to heaven because of their faith in Jesus, not because of works. But when it comes to everyday life, they keep trying to perform up to God's standards, and, of course, they quickly discover they cannot.

HIS LIFE IN US

Jesus didn't die to help us perform better. He died and rose again to live His life through us. That's what Galatians 2:20 is all about: "I have been crucified with Christ and I no longer live, but Christ lives in me. The life I live in the body, I live by faith in the Son of God, who loved me and gave himself for me."

Let me tell you something: It's not hard for us to live the Christian life; it's *impossible!* Only Christ can live the Christian life, because the Christian life is living up to God's standards. "Be holy, because I am holy," God tells us (1 Peter 1:16). And we look up in desperation and say, "Yeah, but I'm not God. How can I be holy? That's mission impossible." And that is absolutely true.

But here's what we've got to understand. Christ rose again to live His life in us. We don't have to do it because we *can't* do it. It is His resurrection life inside of us that enables us—empowers us—to be able to live the way God wants us to live.

That means I no longer have to live with this driving need to perform for God. I simply have to allow the power of Christ in me to live His life through me. Jesus said, "I am the vine; you are the branches. . . . Remain in me and I will remain in you. No branch can bear fruit by itself; it must remain in the vine. Neither can you bear fruit unless you remain in me. . . . Apart from me you can do nothing" (John 15:5a, 4, 5b).

If you cut a branch off the vine, it can no longer continue to bear fruit. The branch is useless unless it's attached to the vine. If it is attached to the life-giving vine, what does it have to do to bear fruit? Work hard at it? Can you hear a branch saying, "Oh, I really have to do a good job at bearing this fruit. I must perform better than the other branches in order to bear good fruit."

No, all that branch has to do is to stay attached to the vine so that the life-giving sap flows from the vine to the branch. The fruit then happens automatically. It is inevitable as long as the branch is attached to the vine. The branch is nothing more than a fruit hanger!

We are the branches. What's our job? Stay attached to Jesus. Stay close to Him. Get to know Him. Let His life flow from the vine into us. And then the fruit appears.

ABIDING IN JESUS

What does it mean to "abide in Jesus"? "If you abide in My word, then you are truly disciples of Mine; and you shall know the truth, and the truth shall make you free. . . . If therefore the Son shall make you free, you shall be free indeed" (John 8:31–32, 36 NASB).

First, we must abide in His Word. Then we'll know truth—and truth will set us free from living in a performance-driven mode. Remember, Jesus and the Word are the same thing. John 1:14 tells us that the "Word became flesh and made his dwelling among us." When we abide in the Word, we abide in Jesus, and vice versa. God does not reveal truth contrary to His written Word, but neither does He want His people to become experts in the Bible unless their goal is to know the person of Christ, who is the living Word.

So abiding in His Word is more than just intellectual knowledge of what the Bible says. The truths of the Bible are a mystery unless we have the Spirit of Christ to reveal them to us.

Suppose you and I were looking at a dead man who had cancer. In order to solve his problems, what would we have to do? First, we would have to bring him back to life and then cure him of cancer—right? What if we just brought him back to life, but he still had cancer? He would soon die again, of course. What if we cured his cancer but didn't bring him back to life? One without the other would be no good.

When Jesus redeemed us, He brought us back to life *and* cured us of the cancer of sin. He did the whole job. That means I can rest assured that when I die, I'll go to heaven and live there with God forever. But it also means that while I'm still here on earth in this body, I've been given the power to live an abundant, overflowing life.

Please get this very clear in your mind. When you are born from above, God forevermore sees you *in Christ.* He sees you as forgiven, holy, righteous, and, yes, a saint. That is who you are in Christ. Now, how do you see yourself? Are you still trying to win God's approval by performing? Why would you go back into that bondage? You've been set free from the performance syndrome.

Romans 8:1 says: "Therefore, there is now no condemnation for those who are in Christ Jesus." Living a performance-driven life is living under condemnation. If you feel guilt-ridden and condemned because you don't measure up, that condemnation is not coming from God, because He said we are no longer condemned. Period. Done.

When Jesus died for your sins, how many of them did He die for? All of them. How many of your sins were in the future when He died for them? All of them. Then, doesn't that mean that any sin you have yet to commit is already paid for and forgiven? It is, and you are no longer condemned by even the sins yet to come.

We don't have to beg for forgiveness. We have been forgiven already; we must simply accept God's forgiveness. Why have we been forgiven? We are cleansed and forgiven so that we can receive the life of Christ in us. If I am dead, as Paul says I am—"Nevertheless I live; yet not I, but Christ liveth in me" (Galatians 2:20 KJV)—then who has to live my life? Me? No, I'm no longer required to perform. What I must do is allow Christ within me to have complete control so that He can live this new life through me.

NOT SINLESS PERFECTION

Now, I know we don't live sinless lives after we become Christians, because we still are living in these sin-infected bodies. Our *souls* are redeemed, but our *bodies* are not redeemed until we get to heaven. Therefore, I must bring my body under subjection so that it doesn't live contrary to the life of Christ within me. We must reckon ourselves dead to the sins our bodies want to commit.

But what we have as new creatures in Christ Jesus, with this life of Christ in us, is the power to have victory over the sinful urges of our old bodies, our old selves. We don't *have* to sin. We still do it, but not because we can't stop ourselves—only because we haven't learned or haven't been willing to submit to the power of Christ within us.

When you and I choose to sin, the consequences are included, whether we like it or not. You may choose your sin, but you can't choose the consequences. Jesus has delivered us from the penalty and judgment of our sins, but He has not delivered us from the consequences. Therefore, we may be living with some *consequences* of past sin. But we don't have to live under the *condemnation* of those sins.

GROWING IN GRACE

When you and I sin as Christians, when we know we've disobeyed, we have to simply stop it and ask God to show us His grace once more and put us back on the right path. I have begun to notice that when I find I am not performing up to what I know I should as a Christian, I'm no longer surprised. I'm not pleased with myself, but I'm not shocked to discover that when I start to live this life in my own power, I'm going to sin. I have less and less faith in myself and my ability to perform. I know how quickly my performance breaks down.

But I have more and more faith in Jesus and His power in me, and I'm learning to grow in this grace. You see, what we're talking about is living not under the Law, but living in grace! This is all free grace—and we're told that grace is something we must grow in. That means that through getting to know Jesus better and better and reckoning myself dead to sin but alive through Jesus, I can see progress in my spiritual life. That is growing in grace. But it's not performing up to God's standards.

ATTACH YOURSELF TO THE VINE

My friend, Fran, has a childlike faith that has always been an example to me. She simply believes what Jesus tells her and has a very personal relationship with Jesus. She tells me of the time when she learned
that she didn't have to perform for Jesus.

For many years she taught a monthly Bible study in our church
in New York. On one particular morning, the morning of her monthly meeting, there was a terrible scene in her home. She and her husband had an argument and he left in a huff. Then the kids were at
each other's throats, and she yelled at them before they left for school.
And as she stood at the sink trying to wash the breakfast dishes, tears
started pouring down her face.

"Lord," she said, "I can't go teach this class today. Did you just
see how I treated Dick and the kids? Lord, I just can't teach it. I'm
not worthy to teach this class." And in that still, small voice, the Lord
said to her, "Frances, you never were worthy to teach that class. I've
been waiting for you to realize that."

In that moment she grasped the truth that the Christian life she
was trying to live was not one of her performing up to God's standards.
It was one of her giving up trying to perform and understanding that
only as she attached herself to the Vine and allowed His life to perform in her could she ever do anything for Jesus.

Of course, that's not a lesson you learn once in life, and that's it.
We all have to keep relearning it, because we are continually inundat-
ed with the performance-driven mentality the world thrusts upon us.

At another time, years later, she had inherited her mother's diamond ring, and she very proudly wore it. It was a lovely stone, but
the jeweler had told her the stone was loose and needed to be tight-
ened. However, she didn't bother at the time, and sure enough, a few
weeks later she looked down and realized her diamond was missing.

In her simple way, she prayed that God would help her find it,
and she began to search. She really believed God was going to lead
her to that diamond, wherever it was, and of course it could have been
in a million places. But, as she started to look, the enemy started working on her. "How dare you ask God to help you find that diamond! You
don't deserve to find it. After all, you knew the stone was loose. It's your
fault. God's not going to help you find the diamond."

But she stood right up to the Enemy, rebuked him, and said, "Listen, Satan, I know I don't deserve to find that diamond, but I never deserved to have it in the first place. It was a gift from my heavenly Father, and He doesn't reward me according to what I deserve. He will help me find that diamond, even though I don't deserve it."

That inner voice told her to go look in the car, which she did—and you guessed it, she found the diamond. A miracle, and she was glad to have the diamond back. But God was more interested in the lesson she learned and the simple trust she showed in her heavenly Father.

Of course we don't deserve anything from God, but there's no way you're going to change that by performing better and better. The standard is too high; it's unachievable. The Christian life is not difficult; it's impossible! So give up trying.

ALLOW THE LIFE OF CHRIST TO FLOW IN AND THROUGH YOU

Rest in who you are in Jesus, not in what you've done. Throw off the guilt and condemnation you've been carrying around. Some of us stay in guilt because we think feeling guilty will help restore us to God! God doesn't want you to feel guilty. He is not condemning you; He is training you and growing you to be more and more a vessel for Jesus to live in with complete freedom.

Since I am "in Christ," God sees me as righteous, because I've been given the righteousness of Jesus. I'm in line to inherit all of God's riches; I am a coheir with Jesus. I am seated in heavenly places. That's how God sees me.

GOD'S UNCONDITIONAL LOVE

God doesn't love me when I'm good and punish me when I'm bad. That's our kind of human love. But God loves me completely, no matter what I do. God will never love me more than He does right now. My performance will not change His love. His love for me is total. I don't get more of it by performing better. That's the way we humans are, but not God. His love for us is 1 Corinthians 13 love:

God is always patient with you; God is always kind to you. God is not rude to you; He is never easily angered with you. God keeps no record of your wrongs. God does not delight in evil but rejoices with the truth. He always protects you, always trust you, always hopes the best for you, always perseveres with you. God's love for you never fails.

And no matter what you've done, how you see yourself, what you think about yourself, or what you do in the future, His love for you will be just like that, no more, no less. You don't have to perform to earn it. It's yours, right now.

When you don't live by this truth—that you are accepted with or without the performance, just like you are—you will become a "double-minded person," who, James 1:8 tells us, is "unstable in all he does." You've got a split mind about who you are. Yes, you've been born again and you know that is a gift from God, but on the other hand, you keep trying to prove you're OK to get rid of those images from the past, so that you can feel you have earned God's approval.

KNOW YOURSELF BY KNOWING GOD

Here's an important truth: If you want to get to know yourself, get to know God. Don't study psychology or look to the latest theories or counselors to define who you are or to establish your self-worth. Since Galatians 2:20 says we no longer live, but Christ lives in us, why do you need to get to know a dead person? Get to know Christ, who lives in you, and I guarantee you will know what you need to know about who you are.

Paul had a great struggle in Romans 7 about who he was. You remember the passage. "For what I want to do I do not do, but what I hate I do" (v. 15). He was at that point a double-minded man, unstable in all his ways. "Who am I?" Paul asked. Where did he find the answer? By digging up the past and learning more about Saul, the person he once was? No, his solution was to accept the rescue brought about by Christ. "Thanks be to God—through Jesus Christ our Lord!" he proclaimed in gratitude (v. 25). And he went on to declare, "Therefore, there is now no condemnation for those who are in Christ" (8:1). There was now no condemnation for Paul.

If you are bound up today in trying to perform to God's standards or anyone else's, you're living in legalism and in error. If truth sets us free, error binds us. Galatians 5:1 says, "It is for freedom that Christ has set us free. Stand firm, then, and do not let yourselves be burdened again by a yoke of slavery."

If you know Jesus as your Savior, you're free.

You've heard the story of the man walking down the road with a heavy, heavy burden on his back. So heavy he could hardly move. A farmer came along in a truck and offered him a ride. So the man jumped into the back of the truck with his heavy burden and the farmer drove off. After a few miles, the farmer looked in his rear-view mirror and saw that the man was sitting in the truck with that heavy load still strapped to his back. He stopped the truck and said, "Why are you still carrying that load? Why don't you put it down?" And the man said, "Oh, I couldn't impose on you like that; it's enough you're giving me a ride. I couldn't ask you to carry my burden, too."

And many of us are doing that in our Christian lives. We're on the truck that's taking us to be in heaven with Jesus; our destiny is settled. But we refuse to commit our burdens to Jesus; we keep trying to perform and carry everything ourselves. When Jesus saved you and put you in the truck, He intended that you put down the heavy burden of living in a performance-driven world and allow Him to become your life.

STOP FLAPPING

Keep the flapping eagle in your mind and remember that flapping will bring you down. You can't flap and soar. Let the wind of God's Spirit take you to new heights; rest in the assurance of His unchanging love; pray for your growth in His grace so that you become more and more like Jesus; and then enjoy the ride. You were born to soar, not to flap.

THE EAGLE'S MATING RITUAL

There was a period in my single life—and I am still single—when I was in the manhunt mode. I am sure most of my readers have been there and done that, though for you men it would have been the womanhunt mode. Most of us have a very natural desire to find a mate at an appropriate time in our lives and settle down to that ideal married life we've dreamed of for so long.

While in that manhunt mode, I remember making a conscious decision that I wanted to find a man who would love me more than I loved him. The origin of that resolve—which now seems a little arrogant—began as my girlfriend and I lamented the fact that women were so prone to make a fool of themselves over a man. We kept noticing that men were "cool" when it came to relationships, as though they could take us or leave us, whereas we women were more often in the desperate mode, clinging on for dear life.

Feeling that this was not an appropriate or healthy way to establish a relationship, we decided between ourselves to find men who would love us more than we loved them. In retrospect I can tell you that our lofty intentions were often abandoned, since the truth was we were both desperate to find a man!

That kind of manhunt or womanhunt is destined for disaster. It is based more on emotions, hormones, culture pressure, family influence, and ticking biological clocks than on rationale, reason, and objectivity. I'm not convinced that arranged marriages are better, but surely the visceral way we pursue a mate in our society cannot be the best method to find a successful relationship that will make it for the long haul.

The eagle has much to teach us, especially those who are still single, about finding a mate.

THE EAGLE'S MATE HUNT

The female eagle is very particular about choosing a mate. She has a long-term perspective and actually auditions any male eagle who shows an interest in her. You see, eagles mate for life, and she knows that once the romance is over, life begins—and she wants an eagle "husband" who is going to be a good provider, a good father, and a trustworthy mate for many years.

Eagles begin to live on their own when they are about one year old. For the next couple of years, the eagles do what eagles do: soar, hunt for food, build nests, and generally mature into full eaglehood. Then instincts start to take over and the male eagle has the urge to find his mate. Like all men through the ages, he looks around until he sees a lady eagle who catches his eye—a looker, if you please! Once he has spotted the eagle of his dreams, he begins a courting game that could last for days.

This courting exercise begins with the male eagle following after the female relentlessly. He soars along behind her, never giving her a moment to herself. She is savvy and recognizes that he has set his feathers for her, so she plays the game along with him.

If the female eagle decides that he looks as though he could be an acceptable mate, after a few days of tag, she invents her own game. The female dives to the ground and picks up a stick in her talons. With the male eagle right on her tail, she flies back up to a height of eight to ten thousand feet, flying in a figure eight with wide circles and curves. Then, without warning, the female drops the stick and the male attempts to retrieve it for her, catching the stick before it hits the ground. If he is successful, he brings it back to the female, expecting some kind of reward for his demonstration of skill—but she appears to be unimpressed.

Not being easily discouraged, he continues to follow the female, and soon she will do the same thing again. This becomes a series of challenges the female poses for the male eagle. With each drop of the stick, she flies to a slightly lower altitude with a slightly larger stick. This means it drops faster and the male's abilities are thoroughly tested.

If the male ever fails to catch the falling stick, the female will chase him off and refuse to play any more. Perhaps she will allow him to try again at another time, but she rebuffs his romantic pursuits at that time if he doesn't pass muster! One dropped stick is all it takes to cross him off her list.

The game climaxes when the female is about five hundred feet from the ground and has a stick the size of a small log! If the male catches that large stick from that short height, he passes her test. From the chapter on flying lessons, you can see how this test demonstrates the male eagle's ability to be a good father, and that is most important to the female.

Then they actually go through a ceremony of sorts. Vows are made at a high altitude by locking talons together and turning head over heels, thus signifying their intention to begin their life together, and they are together from then on, for the rest of their lives.

CHOOSING MATES CAREFULLY

Indeed, the female eagle seems to have better sense than most of us human females when it comes to making a decision about a mate. She looks down the road at what life is going to be like with that male eagle five years from now, ten years from now, because she fully intends to mate for life. Therefore, she wants to make certain that this mate has the qualities and skills to be the kind of eagle with whom she wants to spend the rest of her life.

Notice that she allows the male eagle to do the pursuing. In our women's lib society, that seems to have become passé. I am told that girls chase boys quite freely from high school years on up and, in fact, are often more aggressive than the boys. Well, it's a huge mistake, women. If you really want to find the right mate, you will let the man do the pursuing. God created us that way, and no amount of liberation will change it. The man wants to be—and should be—the pursuer.

Not fair, you say? OK, go ahead and do it your way. But you won't be happy with the results. You'll cut off your nose to spite your face, believe me. Learn from the eagle: let him do the chasing.

BECOMING "MATABLE"

Note that eagles do not begin looking for mates as soon as they are independent. They give themselves time to mature, develop skills, and make themselves "matable," if you will. There is no eagle dating that goes on here. There is no need to try the field and have many intimate relationships with many other eagles before choosing the right one. The eagle's instincts tell him that when the time is right, when he is "matable," he will look for, find, and marry that mate quickly. But until then, the eagle fixes his mind on becoming an accomplished eagle.

Our dating practices are recipes for regret. Often young people will start dating in their early teens, having many relationships through high school, college, and afterwards, before they are ready to mate. Often these relationships are very close and intimate, even sexual (yes, even among Christians). With each broken relationship we create for ourselves suitcases of regret that we carry with us into the next relationship and eventually into marriage, if and when that happens.

Speaking as a female, I am amazed at how willing we women are to jump through male hoops in order to have a relationship. Going without a man on our arms seems like the worst plague ever inflicted on womankind, and we often abandon all good sense, not to mention moral standards, just to have some kind of male relationship in our lives.

The smart single person—male or female—will first determine when he or she is "matable." At what point in your life are you truly eligible for marriage? Some typical guidelines:

- Is your education completed?
- Have you established some financial stability and lived independently for at least a year?

- Have you pursued some of your dreams that likely won't be possible once you're married (teaching English in China for three months, backpacking over Europe for a summer, working for the Peace Corps for two years, taking a short-term missions assignment—ad infinitum)? These pursuits will develop you as a person in wonderful ways and give you that sense of realizing your dreams, so that you don't go into marriage feeling as though you've missed out on something you really wanted to do, and now it's too late.

Think of what you want to do that would best be done before marriage. Think of who you want to be before you are married. Then choose a time frame when you will have reached those goals. It could be a certain age or a certain point. That would be your "matable" time.

Now comes the hard part. Determine that you will not develop intimate, close relationships with the opposite sex until you are at or near that "matable" time. That most likely will mean no dating, or certainly no steady dating. It will, however, include many friendships with many different people, which will allow you to objectively think about the mate you want. And then once you know the kind of mate you want, you will have time to become the person that man or woman would want to marry.

I will choose not to go into a lengthy discourse here on sexual purity. Suffice it to say that the Word of God is explicit, and no amount of rationalizing ("We're in love"), or shifting blame ("Everybody's doing it"), or making excuses ("We plan to be married someday") will change God's law about sex. Sexual intimacy is reserved for marriage only. When you break that law, you always pay a very high price for it.

Remember that we always reap what we sow, though we reap in a different season than we sow. The sexual promiscuity that seems so good right now and is so acceptable in our society will reap a harvest later on—a harvest of regret and shame and many other potential problems. These include but are not limited to unwanted pregnancies, sexual diseases, abortions, ruined reputations, and a damaged testimony for Jesus Christ.

God's principles are there for our good, our protection. God is not old-fashioned. He is the ever-present God, Alpha and Omega, beginning and ending. He is never out-of-date, out of touch, or out of line. Neither are His principles and commands difficult: "This is love for God: to obey his commands. And his commands are not burdensome" (1 John 5:3).

Keep in mind that you have an enemy who is an accomplished liar, and he bombards you with lies about God all the time. One of his most frequently used and most successful lies is that God's way is out of step and difficult and unreasonable and unnecessary. It's a lie, pure and simple, and if you will refute it with God's Word and choose God's way, you will win—big time!

Take it from the eagle: Don't rush into mating and marriage. You may be thinking that people are marrying much later in life these days, so that's not a problem. That's true, but we rush into intimate relationships long before we are "matable," and that creates problems and regrets that will last our whole lives.

MATE CRITERIA

My manhunt criterion—finding someone who would love me more than I loved him—was not a particularly admirable one and certainly not well motivated, and for sure it was far too brief. I needed to give it much more careful thought and to establish biblical standards that would govern my choice of a mate.

Every unmarried person would be well served to determine his or her mate criteria *before* the mating season begins. This lifelong decision is the most important we ever make, outside of our decision to accept Jesus Christ as the Lord and Savior of our lives. We should give it at least as much careful, rational, prayerful consideration as we do our choice of a college, career, or summer vacation!

I'm not recommending that you put potential mates through some exhaustive qualification exercise, nor that you carry a check list with you on dates, but it would be extremely wise to put down on paper what you want to find in a mate. Once you've done that, go to a trusted advisor, someone who is older and wiser, spiritually mature (preferably), happily married, and knows you pretty well. Show that person your list. Ask for his or her input.

Here are some Bible-based suggestions to give you a start.

- *Does this man have the potential of being the spiritual head of our home?*

This is more than just a Christian man, someone who professes faith in Jesus Christ and attends church regularly. It is a man who pursues God, who places his relationship with the Lord Jesus above all others, and who has a growing faith. "Wives, submit to your husbands as to the Lord. For the husband is the head of the wife as Christ is the head of the church, his body, of which he is the Savior" (Ephesians 5:22–23).

Ask yourself how many Christian marriages you know where the husband takes strong spiritual leadership. Such a husband initiates family devotional time, insists on Christian principles in the home, and is a leader in Christian activities. You may not be able to think of too many men in this category, but this is the kind of man you want to look for.

• *Will this man love me just as Christ loved the church?*

The apostle Paul wrote, "Husbands, love your wives, just as Christ loved the church and gave himself up for her" (Ephesians 5:25). Not only is this a God-focused, Jesus-loving, Bible-believing man; it is also a secure man, someone who doesn't have to prove his manhood or demonstrate his authority.

As I write this, I have just answered a letter from a listener to my radio program who told me a sad, but all too common story of a husband who treats her with disrespect and a heavy hand. He is a Christian husband—in fact, a pastor—but his interpretation of this Ephesians passage is that it gives him all authority over his wife, and she is to accept anything he says or does without question.

Reading her letter I wondered, *Did you not know this about him before you married him? Surely there were some indications in his life and behavior beforehand that would have given you a clue to this unbiblical attitude.* A man who loves his wife the way Christ loves the church would never treat his wife the way this woman was being treated.

Yet, from the tone of her letter, it would appear that she was shocked to discover what she had married. He was a Christian—on staff at a church, even. How could this be a bad choice for a marriage partner? Perhaps that was her only criterion for a mate, and now she is living with the consequences of her poor decision. At this point she has poor prospects for ever having the godly marriage she so wants.

• *Is this woman more interested in being godly than in being glamorous?*

I recognize how important the exterior is to you guys, and that's OK, provided that is not your single or highest consideration. Here is what the apostle Peter wrote about being a godly woman: "Your beauty should not come from outward adornment, such as braided hair and the wearing of gold jewelry and fine clothes. Instead, it should be that of your inner self, the unfading beauty of a gentle and quiet spirit, which is of great worth in God's sight" (1 Peter 3:3–4).

That gentle and quiet spirit Peter refered to is unfading. It will last through the years, whereas looks and sizes and shapes and hair color will not. I would also point out that Peter's reference to a quiet spirit does not mean *wallflower.* Women come in different personalities, just like men, and some women were created by God to be leaders and entrepreneurial. All women have minds and opinions that are equal to men's and worthy of consideration. So a woman can have a gentle spirit even though she is vocal and active.

• *Does this woman understand and agree with the biblical directive of submission?*

The apostle Paul wrote: "Then they can train the younger women to love their husbands and children, to be self-controlled and pure, to be busy at home, to be kind, and to be subject to their husbands, so that no one will malign the word of God" (Titus 2:4–5).

Today this idea of the submissive and subjective woman has been maligned and avoided and criticized and altered. It doesn't sit well with our modern culture of liberated women. I have to admit that my first reaction to this teaching was to shun it or rationalize it away. But it's in the Bible, and we don't have to be afraid of anything that is in the Bible. It was put there under divine inspiration for our good, not for our harm. God's principle is that a married woman is to be in subjection to her husband. Of course, that's not hard to do if you have a husband who loves you as Christ loves the church!

Books have been written on this topic, and it is neither wise nor necessary for me to comment any further. But suffice it to say that submission should not be viewed as a license for a man to rule with an iron fist. When taken in the entire context of Ephesians 5, Titus 2, and 1 Peter 3, the right woman will be willing to acknowledge the male leadership in the home, and the right man will be willing to solicit and respect and consider his wife's opinions and desires. In fact, he will give them first place whenever he can.

A woman who has feminist tendencies, pent-up resentment toward men, and is out to prove that she is "as good as a man" is the equivalent of a macho man who has to prove he is in charge. Neither of those stereotypes fits the biblical principle of each of us putting others ahead of ourselves and being servants.

In Ephesians, Paul wrote, "Submit to one another out of reverence for Christ" (Ephesians 5:21). In Philippians, he wrote: "Do nothing out of selfish ambition or vain conceit, but in humility consider others better than yourselves. Each of you should look not only to your own interests, but also to the interests of others" (Philippians 2:3–4).

• *What kind of parent might this potential mate be?*

Watch how the one you are interested in interacts with children. Notice if this person pays attention to children and how children react to him or her.

• *What is the background of this potential mate?*

That includes his or her cultural background, educational background, religious upbringing, and current relationship with family members. The more opposite you are in these areas, the more difficult will be your "nest-building" challenge. Although differences in any of these areas should not necessarily have veto power, they are red flags to consider because you can be certain they will be points of struggle as the two of you become one.

• *Will this potential mate be a good provider?*

That certainly doesn't mean the man has to have a lot of money or earn big bucks. But it means that he takes this responsibility very seriously and has the skills, abilities, and drive to take care of his obligations as a husband and father. A woman should demonstrate the ability to be a good home-keeper, to be frugal, and to understand her responsibility in making a house a home.

You will remember in the Old Testament how the children of Israel were continually going against God's law and marrying people outside their faith. God warned them over and over not to marry among the pagan people around them. Yet again and again they chose to do this, and every time it brought hardship and pain on themselves and on their nation.

Mate choosing is serious in God's sight, and we need to be at least as cautious and careful as the eagle is. Mating for life is their intention; it should be ours as well. I doubt that many people marry with the intention of getting a divorce somewhere down the line. But divorce has become so commonplace and acceptable in our society that it looks like an easy way out when marriage becomes difficult.

Whether you are a single woman or a single man, choose the stick you will use as a test for a potential mate. Set some standards in your mind and heart that are nonnegotiable, and before you allow your heart and hormones to become involved, drop some sticks; think down the road; imagine ten years from now what life might be like with that person. See if he or she has the qualities that will last a lifetime.

As the eagles choose a mate, they do so with no thought of abandoning that relationship. It is a lifetime commitment, and that means there is no room for error. Surely with all the benefits we have as people of God—the Holy Spirit to guide us, God's Word to teach us, trusted spiritual leaders to help us—we can learn how to choose a mate that will be God's best for us.

THE EAGLE'S LIFESTYLE

For a ten-year period early in my business career, I did my own thing. I pursued the lifestyle and interests I thought would fulfill me and make me feel good about myself. After all, isn't that what most people think life is all about—feeling good about yourself and living like you want to live?

I bought into that whole philosophy, and in the pursuit of my own self-interests, my lifestyle deteriorated significantly. No longer did I live by the principles of God's Word I had been taught from my earliest years. No longer did I obey what I knew to be the truth of Scripture when it came to how I lived my life. I was more interested in finding that elusive "good self-esteem" and being free to do what made me happy.

I'll never forget a conversation I had with a co-worker during this period. For some reason the subject of church came up, and I told him that I always went to church on Sunday. He gave me a shocked look and said, "You go to church every Sunday? I never thought you were the religious type!"

It was like a dagger to my heart, for he succinctly reminded me that my lifestyle was nothing like a Christian's should be, and in the midst of an immoral and hedonistic society, I blended in with everyone else. My lifestyle gave me away.

Christians are meant to have unique lifestyles. In many ways we should not blend in with the world around us because we've been given the privilege of soaring like eagles. And like the eagle, our lifestyle has to be different if we truly want to soar.

AN EAGLE'S DIET

In many ways the life of an eagle parallels that of humans. Eagles can live to be fifty to sixty years old, particularly if they are in a sheltered environment where they have protection. In the wild, their life span may be reduced by ten years or so. But even that is a long life for a bird.

One of the reasons they live as long as they do is that they are careful about their diet. Eagles spend most of their time each day looking for the right thing to eat. They avoid some of the things other birds will eat—such as decaying animals. Usually the eagle goes after fresh meals, such as fish, which he snatches from shallow waters, and other live animals, such as ducks, coots, muskrats, turtles, rabbits, and snakes. The eagle sets out each day to find what he knows he needs to eat to be healthy, refusing to settle for just anything.

Eagles swoop down to seize their prey in their powerful, long, sharp talons, and they can carry off in flight up to about half their weight.

One woman told me an amazing story about an eagle in Alaska who was looking for lunch one day. A couple traveling with their small Chihuahua dog had stopped at a restaurant, and the woman was walking the dog before resuming their car trip. When the eagle spotted that little dog, he decided it would make a nice lunch. So the eagle swooped down and grabbed the dog with its huge talons and carried it off, never to be seen again. As the story was told to me, the woman was distraught —but her husband was secretly glad because he had never liked that dog anyway!

Well, I cannot vouch for the accuracy of this story, and I'm sure the dog lovers (like me) find it most repulsive. But there are other documented tales of eagles looking for their food and aggressively going after what will be good for them. They are particular about what they eat, and that, of course, contributes to their good health and stamina and long life.

THE CHRISTIAN'S DIET

Surely there is an important lesson here for us as believers. Our diet determines our spiritual health and effectiveness. Please don't worry; I'm not going to write about proper eating habits, although that is a spiritual matter we need to take seriously as stewards of the body God has given us. Instead, I want to remind us of the importance of what we feed our minds and our hearts.

Frankly, I am amazed to see how few Christians are careful about what they allow into their minds and hearts. Movies of any description or rating, television programs portraying immoral lifestyles in positive ways, books and magazines that border on the pornographic— these and more are part of many Christians' lifestyle. And then they wonder why they are vulnerable to temptation and spiritual failure.

If you are going to soar like the eagle, you have to be particular about your daily diet. You can't let down the standards even for a short while, for once you allow garbage into your mind, it will not be easy for you to clean it out. For every hour of garbage you let into your mind, you can count on spending a day or more getting it out.

Many Christians seem to think that their faith in Jesus Christ makes them immune to the effects of mental garbage. *After all,* they reason, *I know what is right and what is wrong. I won't be tempted by watching this R-rated movie. I can enjoy the great acting and the interesting story and let the rest of it just roll off my back.*

Not true. That garbage will contaminate your mind the minute you let it in, and your enemy will use it as an opportunity to keep you from soaring.

The apostle Paul wrote in 2 Corinthians 7:1: "Since we have these promises, dear friends, let us purify ourselves from everything that contaminates body and spirit, perfecting holiness out of reverence for God." I copied out that verse into my prayer journal years ago and have been consistently praying it into my life. I encourage you to do the same. Ask God to show you what is contaminating your body and your spirit. Give Him permission to shine the light of His truth on to your lifestyle and point out the things in your "diet" that will do you harm.

The promises Paul wrote about are found in the last two verses of chapter 6: "'Therefore come out from them and be separate,' says the Lord. 'Touch no unclean thing, and I will receive you. I will be a Father to you, and you will be my sons and daughters,' says the Lord Almighty" (2 Corinthians 6:17–18).

Paul was referring the believers at Corinth to Isaiah and Ezekiel, quoting what those prophets of long ago had admonished God's people to do. They were meant to be a separate people who stayed clear of unclean things. When God's people did that, they were promised to have a Father-daughter or Father-son relationship with God Almighty. The same is true for God's people today. With this great promise, it just makes sense that we keep our lives pure from anything that could contaminate our bodies or our spirits, so that nothing will interfere with our relationship with God.

Another translation paraphrases the idea this way: "With these promises ringing in our ears, dear friends, let us keep clear of anything that pollutes body or soul. Let us prove our reverence for God by consecreating ourselves to him completely" (2 Corinthians 7:1 PHILLIPS).

A good question to ask yourself is this: *How much do I truly reverence God?* This in large part is determined by how well you know God, for the more you truly know God's character and greatness, the more reverence and godly fear you will have. If you don't feel a great deal of reverence for the God of the universe, then it's likely you don't know Him very well, for to know Him is to revere Him.

Living a life separate from the impurities of this world, living on a diet that edifies and builds us up spiritually, abstaining from anything that would smirch our body or soul are the ways we prove how much we revere God. Our diet must be carefully chosen and continually scrutinized if we want to soar like the eagle.

AN EAGLE'S NEST

Several things are unique about how an eagle builds a nest. First, the eagle positions it in a very high place, higher than the nests of other birds. This could be a crag in a rock high up, or a large tree that grows in a high place. The reason for this is threefold: to provide protection from predators or enemies; to provide a good perspective of their environment; and to give them a good launching pad for soaring.

Eagles begin building their nests together after they have mated, and these nests grow to be extremely large and strong. They begin their nests with strong, tough tree limbs, adding smaller limbs and twigs as they progress. Then they make the nest soft by adding down feathers, leaves, and other soft material they have gathered.

They return to the same nests year after year, making necessary repairs and additions, and have been found to stay in the same nest for thirty years or more. Their nests grow to be twenty feet deep and nine and a half feet across. A nest can weigh between one and two tons.

This nest-building takes a great deal of time and attention, and it is a lifelong project. The eagle knows that this nest is her place of security and rest, and therefore she commits a great deal of time, effort, and resources to nest-building and maintenance and repair.

GOD'S WORD OUR NEST

What do we as Christians need in order to have a place of security in our lives, a place of protection from which we can launch our flight and soar in the high places? We need a strong and sure foundation that comes from the Word of God. These passages remind us of how important God's Word is in our lives:

> *You are my refuge and my shield;*
> *I have put my hope in your word.*
> *—Psalm 119:114*

> *Every word of God is flawless;*
> *he is a shield to those who take refuge in him.*
> *—Proverbs 30:5*

> *The grass withers and the flowers fall,*
> *but the word of our God stands forever.*
> *—Isaiah 40:8*

Jesus answered, "It is written: 'Man does not live on bread alone, but on every word that comes from the mouth of God.'" (Matthew 4:4)

Like the eagle, it will take us time to build our nest. There is no substitute, no shortcut method in this process. Each of us must get into God's Word on a regular basis, reading it, studying it, praying it into our lives. That's the nest you need if you want to soar.

Biblical illiteracy is at new heights, they tell us, even among those who call themselves Christians. I was blessed to have been raised in a strong Christian home where I was taught the Word of God from childhood. I took that for granted until I was older, and then I realized how many of my Christian friends did not have that kind of Bible upbringing. Their Bible knowledge was sadly lacking because of it.

But I've noticed that the Christian who is serious about soaring like an eagle finds ways to get the Word of God established as his strong foundation. From taking night courses in Bible schools, to correspondence courses, to daily reading and meditating, this person invests significant time in storing God's Word in his mind and heart.

I'm glad you are reading this book, and I could give you a long list of other wonderful books by Christian authors that would enhance and enrich your walk with God. But nothing can replace the Word of God. My rule of thumb has been that I will spend more time in God's Word than all other reading combined. I don't track that precisely, but I do make certain that God's Word has highest priority over all other reading and study.

How does God's Word become our "nest"? Consider these analogies.

• *It provides protection from our predators and the Enemy.*

Surely you are aware that as Christians we have a natural enemy, Satan, who along with his demons is seeking to destroy us in any way possible. Our offensive weapon is the Word of God, as we read in Ephesians 6. Also, Hebrews 4:12 tells us: "For the word of God is living and active. Sharper than any double-edged sword, it penetrates even to dividing soul and spirit, joints and marrow; it judges the thoughts and attitudes of the heart."

The Word of God protects us from the evil intentions of our spiritual enemy. But you have to know how to use your weapon against the Enemy.

For example, once you know where you are vulnerable to attacks from the Enemy and where you are easily tempted to sin, you need to fortify those areas in your life with God's Word.

A sister in Christ from my church related to me that she struggles with wrong thinking in two areas: sexually impure thoughts and thoughts of condemnation, feeling like a total failure. "How do I conquer this wrong thinking?" she asked me. I told her to find verses and passages of Scripture that specifically related to those two areas of temptation. Then she needed to write those passages on small cards, post them all around, even on her screen saver. Better still, she should memorize them. Then when the temptation for either of those lines of thought came upon her, she should start quoting back the Word of God, using it as a weapon against the satanic attacks.

You will recall that Jesus refuted Satan with Scripture when He was tempted in the wilderness. In order to do that, He had to know the Scripture in advance and be prepared to use that powerful sword. The same is true for us.

When you know how to use the Word of God—to rightly divide it—it will give you protection from the onslaught of your enemy. Believe me, Satan cannot abide God's Word, and he flees when it is thrown into his face.

• It provides a unique perspective of the world around us.

When the Word of God is our safe nest, we are "seated in heavenly places" with a view of the world around us that is quite different from the view at the bottom. Reading and knowing God's Word changes the way you see your circumstances. It alters your attitude toward the people in your life. It allows you to understand and accept situations that were once intolerable to you.

It gives you a worldview like no other. With the perspective you gain while perched on God's Holy Word, you will be amazed at how your stress is reduced. Things that used to drive you crazy don't bother you much any more. People who once irritated you, you now see with pity and sympathy. Circumstances you once thought were intolerable become avenues of blessing in your life, as God turns what was meant for evil into something good.

• *It gives us a launching pad for soaring.*

If you are like me, you may find that at times of high workload or stressful deadlines and duties, you tend to spend less time in God's Word. It is a crazy economy we have, thinking that we can use the time we would have spent in God's Word to get our work done or make our deadlines. This plan always backfires on me, and you'd think I would have learned the lesson better than I have.

Not long ago, after falling into that trap once again for a few days, I got back into the Word of God with the discipline and commitment of my normal routine. How refreshed I was as soon as that precious Word of God began to pour on to my dry heart. Tears rolled down my cheeks as I thought of how foolish it was for me to neglect my time with God. I went out that day soaring, like a new person, refreshed and energized as only God's Word can do.

Psalm 119:16 is a good reminder for us all: "I delight in your decrees; I will not neglect your word." If you haven't been soaring much lately, ask yourself how much you have neglected God's Word. There is always a direct correlation between the two.

THE EAGLE'S SOLITARY LIFESTYLE

An interesting thing to note about eagles is that they don't mix a lot with riffraff birds. They have a solitary lifestyle. You won't find them flocked together with vultures or other lesser birds. They are willing to be different.

Why would they not associate with the other birds? Well, I'm not able to read the minds of eagles, but I can imagine that, for one thing, they just don't have similar interests. Eagles are focused on building nests and soaring high and eating right, and the other birds are on a different plane.

Second, since eagles soar higher than other birds, they are simply spending their time at higher levels. This is not because they're better than other birds, but because they can soar to high levels and at high speeds. It just stands to reason that the others birds are left behind, so to speak.

A CHRISTIAN'S SOLITARY LIFESTYLE

Obviously the analogy between eagles and Christians is not always applicable, but there is a lesson for us here. Although we are *in* this world with the other "birds," we are not to be *of* this world. That will mean that at times our lifestyle will have a solitary or even lonely look to it. If we're soaring with the eagles, we'll find ourselves living in a different stratum from most people around us.

It's most important that we don't see this as some place of superiority, for those of us who have been redeemed from our former lifestyles know only too well that it is only the grace of God that allows us to soar. Nothing good in us gives us eagle's wings; they are gifts from God. So we should never demonstrate any attitude of spiritual superiority or smugness.

But we should be aware that our walk with God can isolate us at times. Paul wrote to the Corinthians: "For we are to God the aroma of Christ among those who are being saved and those who are perishing. To the one we are the smell of death; to the other, the fragrance of life" (2 Corinthians 2:15–16).

That Christ aroma which is ours when we are part of His family is attractive to some and repulsive to others. It will cause some people to want to get closer to us and find out how we can soar like eagles. It will cause others to run the other way, as our soaring offends or convicts them.

Jesus said: "This is the verdict: Light has come into the world, but men loved darkness instead of light because their deeds were evil" (John 3:19). Our solitary lifestyle should not be something we choose. Rather, it should be a result of this fact, that many people don't like light shining into their dark worlds—and Jesus has said that we are the light of the world because we carry His light. If you're soaring like an eagle, you can't keep that light from shining, and that may cause some people to shun, avoid, and even demean you. Remember that Jesus warned us, "In this world you will have trouble. But take heart! I have overcome the world" (John 16:33).

There is another sense in which our lifestyle needs to be solitary, and that is in our choice of influences on our lives. The people we spend time with, listen to, and whose friendship we value will inevitably have an influence in our lives. Therefore, we need to choose our influencing relationships very carefully.

Have you noticed that when we frequently spend discretionary time with people who are not soaring like eagles it is far more likely that we will be brought down to their level than we will be able to raise them to our level? That does not mean that we cannot or should not form friendships with nonbelievers; certainly we should. But it does mean that we should carefully determine whom we allow to influence our thinking, morals, and lifestyle. Even some believers aren't good influences in our lives, sad to say!

There may be people in your life from whom you need to be more isolated because they are adversely influencing you and keeping you from soaring.

"JUST SAY NO"

I doubt that Mrs. Reagan had any idea how famous this line would become when as First Lady she answered a question from a young person who wanted to know how to keep from using drugs when his peers were offering it to him. Mrs. Reagan replied, "Just say 'No,'" and the phrase caught on as a national mantra. The apostle Paul used the same simple approach in writing to Titus:

> For the grace of God that brings salvation has appeared to all men. It teaches us to say "No" to ungodliness and worldly passions, and to live self-controlled, upright and godly lives in this present age, while we wait for the blessed hope—the glorious appearing of our great God and Savior, Jesus Christ, who gave himself for us to redeem us from all wickedness and to purify for himself a people that are his very own, eager to do what is good. (Titus 2:11–14)

This great apostle has never been known for his short sentences, and sometimes you think they will never end. But I believe it was because he was so full of God's grace and joy and had so much he wanted to teach his dear children in the Lord that he found it difficult to find a stopping place as he wrote those words. In this sentence-paragraph, he spoke of much that is important to the Christian's lifestyle.

First, we must learn to say no. If you have tasted of the grace of God, and it has changed your life, that will teach you to say no. You will want to say no. You will be eager to say no. Ask yourself: Do you really want to say no to ungodliness and worldly passions? If not, you might rethink your status before God and see if you truly have eagle's wings, because when the Spirit of God lives within you, that wonderful grace of Jesus makes you want to say no.

Saying no to ungodliness and worldly passions isn't necessarily easy, but it is quite simple. You just say no! "No" when you want to watch something that isn't edifying. "No" when you want to say something that isn't kind. "No" when you want to go somewhere you shouldn't. You just say no to ungodliness—anything that hinders your spiritual life and your walk with God. You just say no to worldly passions—those lusts of the flesh that want to move in and take over.

I find it helpful to talk out loud to myself sometimes and say, "No, Mary, you can't go there!" "No, you can't do that!" "No, don't you dare even think about it!" Just say no—*say* it out loud and learn by God's grace—*because* of His grace which has brought salvation to you—to turn away from your former way of life, from the lifestyle of sin and selfishness that ruled you before.

Second, Paul went on to say we are to live "self-controlled, upright and godly lives in this present age." You may be thinking that it was a lot easier to live a godly lifestyle back then than it is now, but that's not true. Their society was just as plagued with evil and bad influences as ours is today. So even in *this* present age, we are to say no to ungodliness and live a godly life.

In case that sounds like a hard lifestyle to you, a life with no fun or excitement or thrills, let me remind you that this description is a lie the Enemy has perpetuated in our society, and sometimes we buy into it. We seem to think that godly living is no-fun living, when, in truth, it is abundant living. It is living without guilt and shame. It is living without regret. It is a spring of water inside of us, springing up with ever-refreshing joy.

Soaring like an eagle is a different lifestyle for us, but it is life on the highest plane. It is living above our circumstances, not under them. It is knowing in reality the truth that Jesus Christ has come to bring us life "to the full" (John 10:10).

CHAPTER 7

THE EAGLE'S ENEMIES

The eagle is a predator. More species are afraid of the eagle than vice-versa. With its huge talons and large beak, the eagle is designed to triumph over his prey. Eagles are not frequently intimidated by other birds or predators. More often than not the eagle is king of the hill.

Golden and bald eagles mostly hunt for fish, snatching them out of the water or stealing them from another fisher bird, such as an osprey. The bald eagle also goes for rabbits and other small game, even young deer. Eagles are a force to be reckoned with. But the eagle does face natural and man-made enemies.

THE EAGLE'S NATURAL ENEMY

The greatest threat from a natural enemy is to the young eagles in the nest. Because the eaglets are so demanding and needy, the parent eagles are away from the nest much of the day, hunting for food for the family. That leaves the little ones vulnerable to their natural ene-my, the snake. A snake can slither up to the high nests, and those lit-tle eaglets look like an easy kill for a mature snake. However, the eaglet senses any strange movement, and when that serpent gets near the nest, the eaglet begins to screech with all his might—and he can make some noise! Usually at least one of the parent eagles is within earshot of the nest, and this cry from their young will bring them back quickly.

Mama or Papa eagle attacks the enemy in one of two ways, or per-haps both. With their large and powerful beaks, they dive at that snake and peck at it repeatedly. Remember, an eagle can go very fast in a dive, and with the force of his flight plus the power of his beak, a few at-tacks like this will usually take care of the problem.

In addition, the eagle can grab a snake in his talons and control that snake pretty easily. Then by flying to a good height, he can dash or drop that snake against a rock, which is likely to kill it or at least disable it for some time to come.

As for other natural enemies, they are few. Only occasionally will the eagle have to be concerned about attacks from another bird or other animal. The eagle is simply too large, too strong, and too fast, and lives too high for most other predators.

THE EAGLE'S MAN-MADE ENEMY

In our modern society, eagles are more threatened by man-made enemies than anything else. Their population numbers in the United States in the early 1700s have been estimated to have been at 300,000 to 500,000 birds. By the early 1960s, their numbers were reduced to endangered levels of less than 500 pairs. This was caused by the mass shooting of eagles, use of pesticides on crops, destruction of their habi-tat, and contamination of waterways and food sources by a wide range of poisons and pollutants. In addition, many eagles have been elec-trocuted through contact with power lines.

The killing of bald eagles in America was prohibited when the Bald Eagle Act was signed in 1940. The Endangered Species Act of 1973 created additional framework for protection of the eagle and its habi-tat. In 1995 the bald eagle's status was changed from "endangered" to "threatened" for the entire United States, and we are seeing increases in the eagle population in all of North America.

OUR NATURAL ENEMY

A friend once said to me, "I want to live in such a way that when my feet hit the floor in the morning, the devil says, 'Oh, no, she's awake!'" Like any knowledgeable Christian, this friend knows that she has a natural enemy not unlike the eagle—that old serpent, the devil. His mission is to cause believers as much difficulty as possible. He would kill and destroy us if he could, and we are in a spiritual battle with him every day. Here are a few things the Bible has to say about our enemy:

> Be self-controlled and alert. Your enemy the devil prowls around like a roaring lion looking for someone to devour. (1 Peter 5:8)

> Jesus said . . . "He [Satan] was a murderer from the beginning, not holding to the truth, for there is no truth in him." (John 8:42, 44)

> (In comparing himself to his enemy, Satan) Jesus said . . . "The thief comes only to steal and kill and destroy; I have come that they may have life, and have it to the full." (John 10:7, 10)

> And no wonder, for Satan himself masquerades as an angel of light. It is not surprising, then, if his servants masquerade as servants of righteousness. Their end will be what their actions deserve. (2 Corinthians 11:14–15)

These and other Scriptures give us an insight into the nature and character of our enemy. He is ruthless; he is smart; he is deceptive; and he is experienced. But, like the eagle, all believers have been equipped to defeat this enemy. There is no excuse for allowing him to have victory over us. Jesus won the victory when He died for our sins, was buried, and rose again the third day, proclaiming victory over sin and death and hell.

Ephesians 4:27 says, "Do not give the devil a foothold." James 4:7 reminds us: "Submit yourselves, then, to God. Resist the devil, and he will flee from you." Second Corinthians 2:11b says of Satan, "We are not unaware of his schemes."

OUR ARMOR AGAINST THE ENEMY

We've been equipped with the armor of God, which will give us the protection and ammunition we need when our enemy attacks. Let me encourage you to get well acquainted with this passage from Ephesians 6:10–18 (PHILLIPS):

> In conclusion be strong—not in yourselves but in the Lord, in the power of his boundless resource. Put on God's complete armour so that you can successfully resist all the devil's craftiness. For our fight is not against any physical enemy: it is against organizations and powers that are spiritual. We are up against the unseen power that controls this dark world, and spiritual agents from the very headquarters of evil. Therefore you must wear the whole armour of God that you may be able to resist evil in its day of power, and that even when you have fought to a standstill you may still stand your ground. Take your stand then with truth as your belt, integrity as your breastplate, the gospel of peace firmly on your feet, salvation as your helmet and in your hand the sword of the Spirit, the Word of God. Above all be sure you take faith as your shield, for it can quench every burning missile the enemy hurls at you. In all your petitions pray at all times with every kind of spiritual prayer, keeping alert and persistent as you pray for all Christ's men and women.

Paul clearly tells us that if we put on God's complete armor, we can successfully resist all the devil's methods of attack. Have you ever learned how to put on the armor of God? Do you do it on a daily basis? If you don't, you are a sitting bird, vulnerable to enemy attacks, completely unprepared, and headed for defeat.

Consider how we have been equipped for victory over our natural enemy.

THE BELT OF TRUTH

This is not a decorative accessory, as we think of a belt. It is worn for protection against blows to the middle. Only a ruthless opponent aims for a punch around the loins and the middle. But that's the kind of enemy we have.

You will remember that Jesus said that the devil is a liar and the father of lies. His ultimate tactic is to lie to us, and he is an expert liar. We must wear the belt of truth to protect ourselves against his lies.

Putting on the belt of truth means that we consciously look for Satan's lies, asking God daily to help us see his deceptions. He will lie to us in our thought lives, placing deceptive and false thoughts and ideas in our heads. He will lie to us through what we hear and believe from other people and through what we read and see. We must learn to detect his lies.

The Word of God is the basis for determining truth. Therefore, you and I have to spend time in the Word, so that we can distinguish Satan's lies from truth. Remember: he is a very good liar. Many times his lies will sound perfectly plausible and reasonable. Furthermore, his lies will be attractive to our human natures; they will be alluring. The Word of God must become our testing station whereby we determine what is true and what is a lie from Satan. Therefore, the better we know the Word of God, the better we will be able to wear the belt of truth.

We cannot wear the belt of truth if there is falsehood of any kind in our lives. If we do not speak and live truth in our everyday dealings with others, that gives Satan a strong foothold and opportunity to defeat us. He is delighted to see us tell something that is not true, or fail to tell the whole truth. We're in his territory then, and he knows we're on our way to defeat.

THE BREASTPLATE OF RIGHTEOUSNESS

The breastplate of a suit of armor is designed to protect an area of extreme vulnerability—the heart. A wound to the heart is usually deadly. Wearing a breastplate is critical.

How does Satan attempt to destroy the heart? By convincing us that we are total failures, without any redeeming virtues, and with nothing good to offer; by telling us that we can never be anything to God and can never do anything in His service. We know from Scripture that Satan is our accuser: "For the accuser of our brothers, who accuses them before our God day and night, has been hurled down" (Revelation 12:10b).

Satan accuses Christians day and night, and many times he succeeds in convincing Christians that they are worthless because they are so unrighteous and unworthy.

It is true that we have no righteousness of our own to wear as protection. But what Satan does not want us to discover is that we have the righteousness of Jesus Christ available to us to wear as our breastplate. Paul said to the Philippians:

> What is more, I consider everything a loss compared to the surpassing greatness of knowing Christ Jesus my Lord, for whose sake I have lost all things. I consider them rubbish, that I may gain Christ and be found in him, not having a righteousness of my own that comes from the law, but that which is through faith in Christ—the righteousness that comes from God and is by faith. (Philippians 3:8–9)

That's the secret: We wear the righteousness of Jesus Christ. How do we put on this breastplate of righteousness? It begins by daily reminding ourselves, early each day, that though we have no righteousness of our own, we have instead the righteousness of Jesus Christ, which we can claim as though it were our own.

Then when the Enemy starts to accuse you, you stand straight up to him and say, out loud if you can, "Satan, I know that I have no righteousness of my own and that your accusations about me are true. But I'm wearing the righteousness of Jesus Christ, and you have no power against it. Therefore, you must stop accusing me, for I will not succumb to your accusations."

This breastplate has to be the righteousness of Jesus Christ. Our self-righteousness will never protect us. If you think Satan is intimidated by the good things you've done or the good life you have led, forget it. The Bible tells us that all our righteousness is as filthy rags, so trying to impress Satan with what we've done or who we are is like wearing tissue paper for a breastplate. Self-righteousness will never protect you. Only the righteousness of Jesus Christ will avail.

Of course, if your life is harboring any unrighteousness, and you are aware of it, that breastplate won't fit very well. God's imputed righteousness should convict us of the things in our lives that are contrary to His will. Many times we bury our heads in the sand and try to ignore some obvious things in our lives that need to be changed. That is a dangerous way to live, because that unrighteousness you know should be forsaken is leaving you vulnerable to Satan's accusations, and your heart could be critically wounded.

THE SHOES OF PEACE

Why would we be told to put the Gospel of peace on our feet? Wouldn't you think that peace should be worn over our hearts instead of on our feet?

Here's the reason. When you have peace on your feet, nothing can stop you. You can keep going no matter what the circumstances. When you are peaceful, you are not vulnerable to the conditions of the path on which you are walking—to the surroundings or the environment. Fear debilitates, incapacitates, and handicaps us, but peace frees us to keep on keepin' on.

When we accept Jesus Christ as our Savior, we are given peace *with* God. Romans 5:1 tells us, "Since we have been justified through faith, we have peace with God through our Lord Jesus Christ."

But in addition to peace with God, we need to have the peace *of* God, and this is the peace that is missing in the lives of many Christians. When you have the peace of God ruling in your life, Satan is frustrated, for no matter what he throws at you, you don't get riled. This is the peace that passes all understanding—even your own.

Many times I've felt as though I were an outsider looking in at myself, wondering why in the world I felt peaceful when the circumstances called for panic. That is unreasonable peace—peace that is beyond your own reason or understanding. And Satan hates to see it in a Christian, because those sandals of peace on our feet make us strong and give us endurance.

How do you get the peace of God on your feet? Philippians 4:6–7 gives some important guidelines: "Do not be anxious about anything, but in everything, by prayer and petition, with thanksgiving, present your requests to God. And the peace of God, which transcends all understanding, will guard your hearts and your minds in Christ Jesus."

The peace of God comes through prayer. It comes through a consistent prayer life and also through an attitude of prayer. Have you learned to pray at all times about everything? The incredible privilege we have as children of God is instant access into His presence, and we can do that in the middle of a meeting at work, on the phone with a difficult person, in traffic when we are running late—anytime, anywhere, instant access to God. And that access into His presence is our passkey to peace.

The peace of God on your feet will give you perseverance and strength and endurance. It will keep you from being vulnerable to circumstances, people, and events.

THE SHIELD OF FAITH

The Scripture says that with the shield of faith we can extinguish all the flaming missiles of the Evil One. All of them! Here are some examples of the flaming arrows that our enemy throws at us.

• *The flaming arrow of hurt feelings*

Hurt feelings often cause us to quit—to quit communicating with someone, to quit trying to help someone, to quit caring, to sit on the sidelines and pout. Also, hurt feelings usually result in some kind of separation between people; relationships are damaged; bitterness and unforgiveness set in.

It's easy to see why Satan uses this flaming arrow often: it works. It stops us and cripples us, and that's what he's trying to do with his flaming arrows. Ask yourself: Do you get your feelings hurt easily and often? If so, you can be sure that your enemy is shooting those flaming arrows at you and will continue to do so, because he's getting to you.

Proverbs 12:16 says: "A fool shows his annoyance at once, but a prudent man overlooks an insult." That's a good verse to memorize if you get your feelings hurt easily. Ask God to help you learn to overlook insults.

I'm convinced that most of the time when my feelings are hurt it is because I've allowed some small thing to get blown out of proportion in my own mind. Perhaps someone will say something that sounds hurtful. Then I start thinking about it, and the more I think about it, the more I am convinced that the person meant me harm. And with that self-pity thinking taking control of my mind, it's not long before I'm in a major funk, convinced I have been unfairly treated.

Obviously, I understand that some people truly intend to hurt others, and all of us have been through that kind of genuinely hurtful situation. But ask yourself how much of your problem with hurt feelings is self-inflicted. If your feelings are hurt often, my guess is that you are allowing yourself to be hurt. It may be painful, but it is often self-inflicted suffering.

Don't you know the Enemy of your soul is sitting on the sidelines celebrating when he sees how effectively hurt feelings can cripple you? Once a person becomes vulnerable to hurt feelings, it takes little effort on his part to shoot that arrow and demoralize you. You do a lot of his work for him.

How effective are you for Jesus Christ when your feelings are hurt? Whom are you thinking about when your feelings are hurt? How good is your testimony to others when your feelings are hurt? It's an effective flaming arrow, and the Enemy uses it on many people once he learns they are vulnerable.

• *The flaming arrow of lack of contentment*

If the Enemy can keep you discontented with something or someone, he will effectively cripple you. Are there some areas in your life where things are not right? Maybe you're in a job that's really tough, or you're married to someone who is difficult, or you're having health problems. For many, it is discontentment with their financial status or with what they possess. And there are lots of single people discontent with being single.

Sometimes we tend to think that those situations are Satan's flaming arrows, but Satan does not have the power to manipulate our circumstances. Instead he uses his power to try to manipulate and control *us*. Often what he does is shoot the flaming arrow of discontentment at us and wounds us severely by making us continually focused on what we don't have or what we wish would happen.

In Philippians 4:11 Paul wrote: "I have learned to be content whatever the circumstances." Notice that Paul said he had *learned* this lesson. If he had to learn to be content, so do we. And if he managed to learn to be content, so can we.

When you find yourself dwelling on the "if onlys" of your life, wishing you could change or manipulate the circumstances or people in your life, quote Philippians 4:11 when that flaming arrow of discontent comes your way. Hold up the shield of faith. Believing it even if you don't feel it will extinguish that discontented feeling and replace it with acceptance and joy.

• *The flaming arrow of self-centeredness*

Quite frankly, this is an arrow our enemy has had a heyday with in the last couple of generations because we've played right into his hands with our emphasis on knowing ourselves, being ourselves, finding ourselves, self-actualization, self-esteem, and so forth. Much of psychology and psychiatry has aided and abetted this flaming arrow, as people have been counseled to focus on themselves and their pasts.

This flaming arrow is particularly deceptive because much of it sounds good, but our enemy knows that any time we become self-focused, we are handicapped. So he'll shoot the flaming arrow of self-centeredness at us a lot and try to get us to think about ourselves all the time.

One subtle way Satan uses this flaming arrow is to get us thinking that God was created for our benefit. Do you find yourself thinking or saying things like, "My prayers are never answered"; or "God just isn't there when I need Him"; or "I don't understand why God isn't doing this for me"? Not always, but many times that's an indication that Satan has gotten to us with this flaming arrow of self-centeredness.

This may take some readers by surprise, but it's very important that we understand that God wasn't created to make us happy or give us fulfillment. We were created to bring glory to God. I often hear messages by Christians focused solely on how God can help us find healing, what we can do to deal with our pasts, and how God is there to help us be fulfilled and complete. Certainly those are wonderful side-benefits of knowing God, but when they become the focus of our message, we've got the cart before the horse and are opening the door for the flaming arrow of self-centeredness to get through—even through Christian literature and messages.

Jesus said that we find eternal life by knowing God the Father, not by knowing ourselves. Look for the telltale signs that indicate the Enemy is getting to you with this subtle flaming arrow. This is one we really don't see coming, and when it finally hits, it can cripple us for long periods and cause lots of damage to our walk with God.

If self-centeredness is your problem, remember what Jesus told us: "Whoever finds his life will lose it, and whoever loses his life for my sake will find it" (Matthew 10:39). If you really want to find fulfillment and life on the highest plain, stop those flaming arrows of the Evil One with this biblical truth.

• *The flaming arrow of lack of discipline*

Sometimes we laugh at the areas in our lives where we lack discipline, but it's really not a laughing matter. Is there some undisciplined area in your life right now? It's like a flaming arrow in your side, getting in your way and keeping you from total effectiveness.

I know God has been dealing with me about some small areas in my life where the discipline has slipped. To tell you the truth, I'm not crazy about discipline. Are you? I'd rather "doing my own thing," as we say. But when I start neglecting disciplines, even small ones, I find that it leads to painful situations and defeat. Satan will shoot this arrow at you very often, trying to convince you that "you deserve a break today," and doing anything else he can to get you to abandon needed disciplines in your life.

Maybe it's discipline in your eating habits, or discipline in your work habits. Could it be discipline in spending consistent time getting to know God, or perhaps discipline in taking care of your body through appropriate exercise? Think of the lack of discipline in your life as one of those flaming arrows Satan is aiming at you with the goal of keeping you as ineffective as possible.

Here are a few of the many verses in Proverbs to hold up as your shield of faith against a lack of discipline:

> *The corrections of discipline*
> *are the way to life.*
> *—Proverbs 6:23b*

> *Whoever loves discipline loves knowledge.*
> *—Proverbs 12:1*

> *He who ignores discipline comes to poverty and shame,*
> *but whoever heeds correction is honored.*
> *—Proverbs 13:18*

> *He who ignores discipline despises himself.*
> *—Proverbs 15:32*

• *The flaming arrow of negative attitudes*

We sing a lot of Christian songs about joy. "Joy flows like a river." "The joy of the Lord is my strength." "I've got the joy, joy, joy, joy down in my heart." But an awful lot of us have such negative attitudes that the joy of the Lord never shows through.

A few years ago I decided to take a serious look at my negative thinking and talking and bring them under the control of the Holy Spirit. I was amazed to see how often I talked and thought negatively. When the Enemy can get this flaming arrow through to us, he really wins, because a sour, negative attitude is about the worst testimony anybody could ever have, and that suits Satan just fine.

Have you been hit by this flaming arrow? This is one way Satan ruins us on our jobs, by getting us into the complaining and griping mode along with everybody else. Start listening to yourself talk; start analyzing your own thoughts. What are you thinking in your head that nobody else knows about? How much of it is negative?

In Philippians 3:1 Paul wrote: "Finally, my brothers, rejoice in the Lord!" And in Philippians 4:4, he repeated himself: "Rejoice in the Lord always. I will say it again: Rejoice!" Those words were written by a man being held in prison, a man unfairly and unjustly treated. He could have easily complained and griped. Instead he taught the Philippians the power of being joyful always. It is a strong weapon against the flaming arrow of the Evil One.

• *Other flaming arrows*

This is certainly not an exhaustive list of Satan's flaming arrows. He has an arsenal and knows which ones to use against you because he has learned where you are vulnerable. It could be that he shoots doubt your way quite often, causing you to wonder if God truly cares for you and if you can trust His promises. Fear is another common flaming arrow, and that can include all kinds of fear. Fear of the future, fear of dying, fear of failure, fear of rejection—an almost endless list.

When you see a flaming arrow headed your way, hold up your shield of faith. Don't forget that faith comes by the Word of God, so use Scripture to generate and bolster your faith. Say out loud with the apostle Paul: "I know whom I have believed, and I am convinced that he is able to guard what I have entrusted to him for that day" (2 Timothy 1:12). Quote from Isaiah 54:17: "No weapon forged against you will prevail, and you will refute every tongue that accuses you. This is the heritage of the servants of the LORD." Recite David's words from Psalm 56:3–4: "When I am afraid, I will trust in you. In God, whose word I praise, in God I trust; I will not be afraid. What can mortal man do to me?"

You will not be able to stop those missiles unless you hold up the shield of faith. And the strength of your faith is directly related to the priority you give in your life to God's Word. But we have a promise that by holding up the shield of faith, we can extinguish every flaming arrow of the Evil One.

THE HELMET OF SALVATION

We are all aware that our minds are vital to our health, both physically and emotionally. The Bible tells us that we are what we think (see Proverbs 23:7 KJV). Before anything happens outwardly, it has its beginnings in the mind.

Little wonder that Satan makes his greatest effort to control our thinking. If he can capture the mind with his lies, he can control and destroy the whole person. If he cannot control all of our mind, he'll settle for a part of it, knowing once he is there, he can get further. He has the ability to project his thoughts into our minds so that we think his thoughts are our thoughts. He is cunningly deceptive.

Without the helmet of salvation every day as our protection against Satan's onslaught against our minds, we are defenseless.

What does it mean to wear salvation as our helmet?

Protecting our minds with the salvation we have from Christ means that we don't allow anything into our minds that contradicts or violates or offends that salvation. Anything that is not in harmony with our commitment to Jesus Christ and the salvation He has given us should not penetrate our mind.

The rubber really meets the road here. Philippians 4:8 tells us what our thought life should be like: true, noble, right, pure, lovely, admirable, excellent, praiseworthy. The Bible says that we should bring every thought into captivity and "make it obedient to Christ" (2 Corinthians 10:5).

Who is in control of your mind today? Does Satan have some or all of it? You must put on the helmet of salvation by determining to guard closely what goes into your mind and constantly bringing all of your thoughts into captivity.

THE SWORD OF THE SPIRIT

The armor we've discussed so far has been defensive armor designed to protect us from Satan's attacks against us. The good news is we have one offensive weapon in our arsenal, and it is totally sufficient for any battle we may encounter. The Word of God is our sword. Paul wrote in 2 Corinthians 10:3–4: "For though we live in the world, we do not wage war as the world does. The weapons we fight with are not the weapons of the world. On the contrary, they have divine power to demolish strongholds."

Just as the mature eagle will peck its enemy to death or defeat him with fierce attacks and a strong beak, so we can be prepared to attack our enemy with our offensive weapon. The Word of God is "living and active. Sharper than any double-edged sword, it penetrates even to dividing soul and spirit, joints and marrow; it judges the thoughts and attitudes of the heart" (Hebrews 4:12).

Remember how Jesus defeated Satan when He was tempted in the wilderness. Satan tried to trick Jesus by using Scripture inappropriately and out of context. But Jesus knew the Word of God too well for that. He quoted Scripture back to Satan, and though Satan tried three times to trick Jesus, he finally had to give up because the Word of God was far too powerful for him. (See Matthew 4:1–11; Mark 1:12–13; Luke 4:1–13.)

If Jesus had to use the Word of God to defeat Satan, how much more do we? You will remember also that the Word of God was in His head. He knew it and could recall it when He needed it. Does that give you some idea of how to use the Word of God as your sword? You need to know it to use it, and when you know it, Satan has absolutely no defense against it.

You want to really drive Satan nuts? Memorize Scripture. When you memorize it, you have it with you all the time.

Many times our enemy attacks us unexpectedly in the most unusual places, and we don't have time to find our concordance and look up some appropriate Scripture. But when it's in our memory bank, as it was for Jesus when He was tempted, we can whip out that powerful sword and use it against the Enemy to peck at him with the force of God's truth, and he is defenseless against the Word of God.

METHODS OF ATTACKING THE ENEMY

Here are some ideas about other effective ways to peck at that enemy and defeat him whenever he gets near.

• *Faithfulness and steadfastness give us strength against Satan.*

When we refuse to quit or be discouraged, Satan is defeated. Paul told the Christians in Corinth, "It is required that those who have been given a trust must prove faithful" (1 Corinthians 4:2).

I have often gone back to these verses from Isaiah 35 when I felt like quitting: "Strengthen the feeble hands, steady the knees that give way; say to those with fearful hearts, 'Be strong, do not fear; your God will come, he will come with vengeance; with divine retribution he will come to save you'" (vv. 3–4). At this present moment in my own life, I have been challenged to recommit myself to faithfulness. Being a goal-oriented person by nature, I have a hang-in-there type of personality. So sometimes through sheer grit of my will I have hung in there when nothing in me really wanted to.

I thank God for giving me a tenacious personality; it comes in handy at times. But there are times when even my own tenacity fails me, and it is then that I must cry out to God: "Strengthen my feeble hands; steady my wobbly knees. I want to run away, Lord."

That's when we truly learn to walk by faith, not by sight, not by feelings, not by emotions, not by self-esteem. And when the devil sees that we refuse to give in or run away, even when we feel like doing so, he is defeated in our lives, and defeated soundly.

How many people do you know who used to be servants of the Lord but are now sitting on the sidelines or, worse, living a non-Christian lifestyle? I can think of several, and I imagine you can, too. Quitters who run into a hardship and give up; who faced the Enemy of their soul and lost the battle. Note that this has not brought them the fulfillment or satisfaction they were looking for; in fact, they are more miserable than ever.

Don't lose heart. As Jahaziel the prophet said to Jehoshaphat and the people of Judah: "Do not be afraid or discouraged because of this vast army. For the battle is not yours, but God's" (2 Chronicles 20:15).

And remember what David wrote: "For the LORD loves the just and will not forsake his faithful ones. They will be protected forever, but the offspring of the wicked will be cut off" (Psalm 37:28).

• A joyful spirit is anathema to the Enemy.

When we are joyful people, Satan is not a happy camper! Habakkuk knew what it meant to be joyful. He said: "Though the fig tree does not bud and there are no grapes on the vines, though the olive crop fails and the fields produce no food, though there are no sheep in the pen and no cattle in the stalls, yet I will rejoice in the LORD, I will be joyful in God my Savior" (Habakkuk 3:17–18).

It's clear that being joyful does not mean having everything in your life just the way you want it. Habakkuk was in a circumstantial mess, but he said, "Yet I will rejoice in the LORD, I will be joyful in God my Savior."

When the Enemy sees a joyful spirit, he tucks tail and runs. He hates to see you get up in the morning with a joyful attitude. So, frustrate Satan; be joyful.

• Praise silences the Enemy.

David wrote, "From the lips of children and infants you have ordained praise because of your enemies, to silence the foe and the avenger" (Psalm 8:2).

One way to do that is just to verbally praise God all through your days for every good thing. Let me encourage you to get in the habit of praising God verbally any time you have a chance. "I praise You, Lord, for the sunshine." "I praise You for healing my headache." "I praise You for a safe trip." Every time something good happens to you, don't overlook it or take it for granted: Praise God for it. Every time you do, you will be silencing the Enemy. He cannot stand a praising person.

• *A repentant and humble heart is important in defeating Satan.*

Pride is always an open invitation to the Enemy. Any time we have a self-righteous attitude or think we're something, we are very vulnerable to his attacks. Conversely, when we have a humble spirit, Satan has difficulty getting to us.

A. W. Tozer wrote:

> The only sure defense against self-righteousness is to cultivate a quiet state of continual penitence. A sweet but sobering memory of our past guilts and a knowledge of our present imperfections are not incompatible with the joy of the Lord; and they are of inestimable aid in resisting the enemy.[1]

Although God never heaps guilt on us, and when our sins are forgiven they are forgotten by Him, it is nonetheless helpful for us to occasionally recall the pit from which we have been snatched. I often pray Psalm 40:2: "He lifted me out of the slimy pit, out of the mud and mire; he set my feet on a rock and gave me a firm place to stand." It reminds me of where I was before Jesus rescued me, and it humbles me to think of where I would be without Him.

That kind of thankful memory does not cause me pain or guilt but simply keeps me humble. Want to give the Enemy a tough day? Keep a repentant and humble attitude; it will help you immensely in resisting the Enemy.

OUR MAN-MADE ENEMIES

Eagles have more trouble with unnatural enemies than with natural ones. And often that is true for us, as well.

Here's a fairy tale that teaches an important lesson.

A young girl was walking through the woods one day when she almost stepped on a snake. When she saw the snake, she pulled back in horror, but to her amazement, the snake cried out to her, "Oh, I'm so glad you came along. I'm so cold and need a friend. Will you please pick me up and put me under your coat so I can get warm, and will you be my friend?"

In fear, the girl replied, "Oh, no, I can't possibly do that. You're a rattlesnake and you will bite me. I can't pick you up."

"No," the rattlesnake answered, "that's not true. I promise I won't bite you. I really want to be your friend, and after all, am I not a creature of God's, just like you? I'm so cold; please pick me up."

She began to feel sorry for the snake, and sat down to think it over. As she looked at the snake, it became more beautiful to her with its many colors. She noticed its graceful lines and movement, and gradually it began to look harmless to her.

She thought, *Well, he's right after all. God created him. And just because most rattlesnakes bite doesn't mean this one will. It seems like a very nice snake, and shouldn't I be willing to be a friend when someone asks me?*

So, she said, "Yes, I will be your friend," and she picked up the snake and put it under her warm coat. Immediately the snake bit her, and the poison flooded her body. She cried out in pain, "Why did you do that? Why did you bite me? You said you wanted to be my friend."

As the snake wiggled away from her, it turned and with a smirk, said, "Hey, you knew what I was when you picked me up."

This is just a fairy tale; snakes don't talk. But there's a most important lesson for us in that simple story. When something looks attractive to us, how easy it is for us to rationalize away the dangers we know exist. How easily we are deceived into lowering our standards and going down the wrong path because our human reasoning tells us it will be all right.

Sometimes we are our biggest enemy! We make our own problems by ignoring the red flags, pushing the envelope, straying off the path a bit here and a bit there. And in our society, where it seems all the rules have changed, it is easier than ever to be duped by a man-made enemy. Just as eagles are facing deadly threats to their lives because of pollution and other things caused by our society, so we face all kinds of soul-pollution blaring at us from our television sets and movie screens, headlining our magazines and newspapers, and handed down to us in new social norms and abandonment of moral integrity and responsibility.

Just as the eagle of a hundred years ago never faced the dangers of today's environment, so we are facing dangers unknown a generation or two ago. I remember talking with a lovely woman who had allowed herself to be deceived into a sexual relationship with a man. He had treated her kindly, and at that point in her life she was vulnerable to kind treatment. It felt good. Then, when he invited her to spend a weekend with him and sent the airline tickets, it seemed exciting and flattering to her. She chose to ignore the obvious dangers that lay in following this path.

She never intended for the relationship to become immoral; she thought they could simply enjoy a weekend together—alone. But she had picked up a rattlesnake, though, of course, she wanted to believe it was a harmless, friendly animal. But it wouldn't take an expert to know that she was playing with a rattlesnake. The signs were obvious; she chose to ignore them because at the time it appealed to her. But later on she had to deal with the pain and the poison that were the aftermath of that relationship.

That was a man-made enemy that women of a few generations ago seldom faced because that kind of behavior was so unacceptable. Now, everybody's doing it; there's no shame in illicit sexual relationships; and even Christian women fall into the man-made cesspools that are everywhere.

> *Let your eyes look straight ahead,*
>   *fix your gaze directly before you.*
> *Make level paths for your feet*
>   *and take only ways that are firm.*
> *Do not swerve to the right or the left;*
>   *keep your foot from evil.*
>   *—Proverbs 4:25–27*

> *There is a way that seems right to a man,*
>   *but in the end it leads to death.*
>   *—Proverbs 14:12*

Don't Talk to a Snake

When you think of our fairy tale, the first mistake the girl made was to talk to that snake. When you see a rattlesnake, there's really no need for a discussion. You know its nature, you know it's not going to change, so you don't stop to talk; you run away as fast as you can.

Jesus said, "If your hand causes you to sin, cut it off. . . . And if your foot cause you to sin, cut it off. . . . If your eye causes you to sin, pluck it out (Mark 9:43–47). That sounds drastic, doesn't it? Jesus was definitely trying to make a strong point, and this is it: It is better to be minus a hand or a foot or an eye than it is to allow ourselves to be caught in sin and led into wrong paths.

The eaglet sets up a scream that can be heard for miles at the first indication that an enemy is getting near the nest. As soon as he senses any strange or foreign sound or smell, he moves—and moves fast—to get help. If he waits until he can see the enemy, it is too late. Mom and Dad eagle won't have time to get back and save him.

I think it is at the initial stages that we make our most serious mistakes. Early on in the process of temptation, when first we are confronted with the rattlesnake, we have the opportunity to get away from it. But so often we make the mistake of thinking we can play around with it just a little bit, never intending to pick it up.

That's where our problems start. When you see a rattlesnake, remind yourself that there is no safe territory with this thing. The Bible says that when we think we're standing, we're most likely to fall. When you find yourself thinking, "I can handle this," or "I'll just go so far and no further," then you know you're talking to that rattlesnake. Don't allow the temptation to go any further. As soon as you see it, run.

In 1 Corinthians 10:13 we read: "No temptation has seized you except what is common to man. And God is faithful; he will not let you be tempted beyond what you can bear. But when you are tempted, he will also provide a way out so that you can stand up under it."

When you encounter a rattlesnake, you can be certain there is a way out. If you'll move fast, God has provided a way of escape. The problem is that all too often we are attracted by the rattlesnake and hang around too long, and then the trapdoor is shut and we've missed the way of escape.

KNOW A LIE WHEN YOU HEAR IT

The second mistake our friend in the fairy tale made was to listen to the lies of the snake. His lies sounded reasonable to her. He even used God in there somewhere to deceive her into thinking he was harmless. As we've already discussed, one thing we know for sure is that Satan our enemy is a masterful liar. He knows how to deceive us with his enticing words.

If she had never stopped to talk to him, she would never have been deceived by his lies. But once she listened, she had difficulty discerning the truth and couldn't think very clearly.

Remember, when you walk into the Enemy's territory, you are inviting deception, because Satan is the father of lies and he's very good at it. He mixes lies with enough truth to stump you. This dear woman who shared her predicament with me was still struggling with the lies that had deceived her. After all, he really was a nice man, and though she knew it was wrong, she kept trying to rationalize it away because it had made her feel good to be treated so kindly.

Oh, do we ever get ourselves into predicaments when we start listening to our feelings. Remember, just because it feels good doesn't mean it's right! Your feelings can lead you so far off the right path, you wouldn't believe it! If that's the kind of rationalizing you've been doing, you're picking up a rattlesnake.

DON'T TELL YOURSELF THAT RATTLESNAKES CAN CHANGE

After she made the mistake of talking to the rattlesnake instead of running away, and then being deceived by its lies, her next mistake was to ignore the laws and principles that are always true about rattlesnakes. When you put a rattlesnake under your coat, when you play in its territory, when you put yourself in places where you know rattlesnakes live, you're going to get bitten because that's the nature of rattlesnakes, and it won't change even for you.

As we've seen so many leaders in politics and religion who have been disgraced by immoral behavior and loss of integrity, we wonder how they could have gotten into such a mess. Well, I think many times they thought the rules just didn't apply to them. They considered themselves above the laws that the rest of us must live by.

Somehow power does that to people. But don't be fooled. Nobody breaks God's principles and gets by with it. If you see people who appear to be doing well while living in rebellion against God's laws, remember that you haven't seen the end of the story yet. No one can live in opposition to God's moral laws and His principles and escape the consequences.

PUT ON JESUS

When an eagle grabs the enemy snake with her huge talons and dashes it against the rocks, that snake is defeated.

Consider our Rock:

> *For who is God besides the LORD?*
> *And who is the Rock except our God?*
> *—Psalm 18:31*

> *My soul finds rest in God alone;*
> *my salvation comes from him.*
> *He alone is my rock and my salvation;*
> *he is my fortress, I will never be shaken.*
> *—Psalm 62:1–2*

> *They all ate the same spiritual food and drank*
> *the same spiritual drink; for they drank from*
> *the spiritual rock that accompanied them, and*
> *that rock was Christ.*
> *—1 Corinthians 10:3–4*

We have a Rock, Jesus Christ. He is our sure defense, and He is the personification of our armor.

- Jesus is truth. We are to put on truth. Jesus said, "I am the way and the truth and the life" (John 14:6).
- Jesus is our righteousness. Righteousness is our breastplate. Paul tells us in 1 Corinthians 1:30 that Jesus has become our righteousness.

- Jesus is our peace. We are to wear peace. Paul tells us that Jesus Himself "is our peace" (Ephesians 2:14).
- Jesus provides our faith. Faith is our shield. In Hebrews 12:2 we are told that Jesus is "the author and perfecter of our faith."
- Jesus is our salvation. Salvation is our helmet. The psalmist said, "The Lord is my light and my salvation" (Psalm 27:1).
- Jesus is the Word of God. We are to take the Word of God as our sword. John 1:14 tells us that "the Word [of God] was made flesh, and dwelt among us" (KJV). Jesus is the Word of God incarnate, God in the flesh.

Do you see again how totally sufficient Jesus is for all of our needs? He is our armor. He is our defense. He is our salvation. All that we need is in Jesus. Just put on Jesus every day.

We have everything we need to be victorious over our enemy, if we will just learn to be prepared. And when we're prepared for the Enemy, he shakes his head when we wake up each day and says, "Oh, no, she's awake!"

EAGLES AND STORMS

It was a one-hour flight from Chicago to Cincinnati, where I would connect with another short flight to Chattanooga to visit my mother. No big deal.

I've flown a lot, spending as much as eighteen hours on oversees flights quite often, so this one was a no-brainer.

But it didn't work out that way. It was one of the most miserable hours of my life, as that airplane bounced and shook in every direction, with many sudden drops and swings, for the entire trip. I white-knuckled it all the way, as did every other passenger on the flight. Sure, I prayed and sang songs of the faith and quoted Scripture as we bounced around, but my knuckles remained white. I was certain no airplane could hold up long under the beating ours was taking.

I remember praying, "Lord, if you'll get me off this airplane safely, I promise, I'll never get on another one." That's how bad it was—and upon arriving in Cincinnati I called my brother to tell him I didn't know if I could board another flight or not.

But I did get on that next plane, with some fear and trepidation, wondering if this flight was going to be an equally frightening experience. The first few minutes were pretty shaky, but soon that plane soared above the storm and we broke through into sunshine. It was hard to believe that all along above the storm there was this wonderful, glorious sunshine. The clouds were beneath us, the storm was below, but our flight was smooth because we were able to fly above the storm.

EAGLES AND STORMS

With their heightened senses, birds are aware of coming storms before people are, as a rule. When they sense a storm on its way, most birds fly off, getting away from the storm as far as possible. Frankly, that sounds like a good strategy to me. The only question is, can they fly fast enough and find shelter soon enough? Sometimes it's just not possible to get out of a storm's path, no matter how hard they fly, and getting caught in the storm can be a death sentence for many birds.

Eagles, however, deal differently with an approaching storm. As with other birds, their senses warn them of a storm well in advance, but they do not try to escape it the way other animals and birds do. Storms don't frighten the eagles because they know they are equipped to deal with them, and they know that the winds of a storm can actually work to their advantage.

An eagle will stay perched on his nest until he feels the first raindrops. Then he launches flight from his lofty home, using the strong winds that accompany the storm to take him higher and higher until he sees the sunlight beams around him and the storm clouds beneath. The eagle has no ability to stop the storm, but he has the ability to fly above the storm.

During a storm if Mama eagle has babies in her nest, she won't leave them. Rather, she stays behind, opens wide her wings and completely covers the brooding area of the nest, keeping the little ones safe from the storm.

THE STORMS OF OUR LIVES

Storms come in all shapes and sizes, and no one is immune from them. While your storm may seem worse than mine, or my storm may last longer than yours, when you are in the midst of a storm, it's of little comfort to think that someone else has been through a storm worse than yours. It's your storm, and it's frightening.

Jesus told us up front to expect storms, and he also told us how to react to them. "I have told you these things, so that in me you may have peace. In this world you will have trouble. But take heart! I have overcome the world" (John 16:33).

He was teaching the disciples about the storms of life they could expect. Knowing that very soon He would return to His Father and that the disciples would be left on earth to spread the gospel, He wanted them to be ready for what lay ahead.

"You will have trouble." It's guaranteed. If you thought that the Christian life meant an escape hatch from trouble, no doubt you've already learned how mistaken you were. If anyone has tried to teach you that being a Christian means prosperity and good health and favorable circumstances, hopefully you have already realized they were not teaching you the truth of Scripture. Jesus warned us that we would have trouble. He surely had His share of it, and all the great heroes and heroines of our faith have encountered all kinds of trouble. Jesus knows all about our troubles. He is never surprised to find that trouble has found its way into our lives. He told us to expect trouble.

"But take heart," He reminded the disciples—and us. "Take heart, be encouraged, don't be sad, because I have overcome the world." We may honestly ask, *What good does it do me in my troubled world to know that Jesus has overcome the world? What does that mean anyway? And how does that bring me comfort or help me deal with my troubles? That's Jesus, and I'm me!*

Here's how it makes a difference. We who are born again by His power are "in Jesus." That is our position, as we discussed in detail in chapter 4.

"I [Jesus] am the vine; you are the branches. If a man remains in me and I in him, he will bear much fruit; apart from me you can do nothing." (John 15:5)

You are all sons of God through faith in Christ Jesus, for all of you who were baptized into Christ have clothed yourselves with Christ. (Galatians 3:26–27)

For you died, and your life is now hidden with Christ in God. (Colossians 3:3)

Since we are in Him, we are able to take heart and be encouraged, even in the midst of trouble, because we don't have to weather the storm; Jesus does it for us. We are in Him, and He has overcome the world and its trouble.

You've experienced that warm, protected feeling you have when a storm is raging outside your window, when the wind is blowing things all over the place and the raindrops seem to be baseball size—and yet you are safe inside. A fire is crackling nearby, you've got your favorite comfortable clothes on, and you can look through the window at the storm, but it can't touch you because you're inside the house.

The analogy is inadequate, but hopefully you get the picture. That's why being "in Jesus" gets us through our storms. He is our protection, and all we have to do—all we *can* do—is to relax "in Him" and enjoy the safety He provides. He won this safety for us when He overcame death and sin and the grave. He rose again to demonstrate His victory over trouble. He is the Master of trouble. He rules over the storms of our lives. He is a shelter in the time of storm.

SOMEONE WITH SKIN ON

Our problem is that we can't physically see or touch or feel the safety He gives us from the storm. It's like the little boy who was afraid of the dark. His dad reassured him that there was no need to be afraid because Jesus was with him. "Yes," he replied, "but I want someone with skin on." In our storms we really want someone with skin on, something we can look at or count or touch. This faith thing is particularly hard when the storm hits.

But when the storms test our faith, we have the opportunity to come out shining like gold.

> *But he knows the way that I take;*
> *when he has tested me, I will come forth as gold.*
> *—Job 23:10*

When the storm has swept by, the wicked are gone,
but the righteous stand firm forever.
—Proverbs 10:25

So we have every reason to take heart because He has overcome this troubled world. It is a done deal, and we can claim His victory in our situations since we are in Him and He is our peace.

OUR REACTIONS TO THE STORMS OF LIFE

Someone has said that when your cup spills over, it reveals what is really inside of you. The storms of life cause us to spill over. I have to tell you from my own life that I have not weathered every storm victoriously from day one. In fact, rarely do I handle storms very well in the beginning.

QUESTIONING AND COMPLAINING

Often my first reaction is to question and complain. I ask, "Why?" "God, this isn't fair!" "God, You don't make sense!" "God, You are not behaving the way I think a god should behave!" Oh, I may not say those exact words, but that's how I feel.

You know, God does not get upset with our "whys." He understands them. In the midst of the storm, we can almost never understand why we are in such trouble. And we beg God to give an account of His actions. David said, "I pour out my complaint before him; before him I tell my trouble" (Psalm 142:2). We should not complain to other people, but God invites us to let Him know exactly how we feel. He knows it anyway, so we might as well verbalize it to Him. You should feel free to tell God exactly how you feel about the storm you're going through.

CRYING FOR THE STORM TO CEASE

A second typical reaction to storms in our lives is to ask Him to stop the storm, to find another way. Jesus did that three times in the Garden of Gethsemane. He said, "My Father, if it is possible, may this cup be taken from me" (Matthew 26:39). He knew the test in front of Him, and He wanted to avoid it if possible.

In the midst of the storm, it's hard to believe that it can work out for our good and the good of God's kingdom. Romans 8:28 is quoted so often it seems like a cliché, and the last thing we want is for someone to quote it. Yet how true it is: "We know that in all things God works for the good of those who love him, who have been called according to his purpose." We think, *Surely there is some other way to do this, something not requiring all this pain and difficulty.*

WORRYING THAT GOD HAS FORSAKEN US

A third response to God's storms is to feel that God has forsaken us. Jesus cried, "My God, my God, why have you forsaken me?" as He hung on the cross (Matthew 27:46). Job voiced the same feelings, found in Job 23:3: "If only I knew where to find him; if only I could go to his dwelling!"

It is natural to think that God could not be in this storm, this awful thing. Like Job, we cry out: "God is not here. I cannot find God. I go where I used to go to find Him—church, daily devotions, Bible studies—but I don't get those good feelings anymore! I'm quite certain if I could just find God and get His ear, this storm would be over immediately." Job said that if he could find God, "There an upright man could present his case before him, and I would be delivered forever" (Job 23:7).

But in the midst of a storm, we often just cannot see or feel God. And it frightens us. Job said, "God has made my heart faint; the Almighty has terrified me" (Job 23:16). He realized he was in the midst of a major test, and he was scared. Maybe you're in that same spot today. You'll find encouragement in Job 23.

WHY TESTING?

Have you ever wondered why God tests us with these storms? Doesn't He know everything about us anyway? Our schoolteachers tested us in part to find out how much we had learned. But God already knows all there is to know about us. So why does He test us?

So That We May Share in His Holiness

Hebrews 12:10 gives us the answer: "Our fathers disciplined us for a little while as they thought best; but God disciplines us for our good, that we may share in his holiness." He tests us for our good, our benefit. I want you to hear those words, especially those of you who right now are in the middle of a tough test and can't see the light. Remember and believe this with all your heart: God is doing this for your good so that you can share in His holiness.

Can you just for a minute look beyond the pain and the problem, and picture yourself being given a piece of God's holiness? Can you see God smiling at you and saying, "Don't fail My test, because I want to give you something very special." How awesome to think that you and I can share in His holiness.

So That We May Know Righteousness and Peace

The writer to the Hebrews goes on to tell us that testing "produces a harvest of righteousness and peace for those who have been trained by it" (Hebrews 12:11). Job said, "I will come forth as gold" (Job 23:10b). In the midst of a terrible test, Job was able to look beyond it and see the end result. Can you do that? I know it's hard, but God wants to encourage you with the assurance that you're going to know righteousness and peace in your life if you will allow this test to train you.

The sad thing is, many of us don't pass our tests. We rebel or run away or try to manipulate the situation instead of accepting it from God's hand and asking Him to use it for His good purposes. If you're going to go through the pain, you might as well know the gain.

And the gain is glorious—a share of God's holiness, righteousness, and peace. That means we become more like Jesus, transformed into His likeness with ever-increasing glory. Just think what a difference that will make in your life. And peace—that glorious peace that passes understanding—is yours when you truly believe that God's test is for your good.

TURNING ADVERSITY INTO OPPORTUNITY

Then, like the eagle, we take those winds of adversity and turn them into winds of opportunity. We fly faster and higher than ever before, carried by the very winds that were threatening our peace, existence, and joy. To use a common vernacular, we "go with the flow," but in this case it is literally true. We go with the flow of the wind of God's Spirit, carried, as it were, to a higher place above the storm.

We admire people who seem to be able to take the lemons of life and make lemonade out of them. I think of the couple here in Chicago, the Reverend Scott Willis and his wife, Janet, who lost six children in a fiery automobile accident caused by a faulty truck ahead of them on an expressway. Their lives were spared, but those six of their precious children who were with them in the van never knew what hit them. That happened in 1994, and their story has been told all over the country.

Our hearts bled as we heard the Willises describe the accident and express their profound sorrow. But they took those terrible, horrific winds of a storm and used them to soar higher. Scott continued to pastor his small church here in Chicago until early in 2000. Like Job, the Willises never cursed God and gave up, as many would have been tempted to do. Instead they continually testified to God's faithfulness through the years of grief, though their "whys" will never be answered this side of heaven.

ABOVE THE STORM OR NOT?

Storms are never easy or fun. There's nothing trivial about a storm, and no need to pretend there is. But what is our alternative? To let the storm wipe us out? To live in bitterness and anger over the storm and its effects? To spend our days mourning and weeping over what could have been or what no longer is? Is that easy?

Easy is a word we should not even consider when we talk about storms. There are no easy ways out. There is just *a* way out. It's not easy to soar on the winds of a storm and rise above it. It takes courage and faith and a denial of your own desire for vengeance and retribution and justice. But your choice is either to soar above the storm and get out of it or to be trapped in its whirlwinds and battered by its torrents. No *easy* here; just above the storm or not.

WHEN THE ANSWER THAT COMES IS UNEXPECTED

Mary and Martha faced a dilemma when their brother, Lazarus, died. You know the story. Lazarus became ill, and the sisters sent for

Jesus to come and heal him. The sisters were confident that Jesus could heal their brother and prevent his death. Not only so, they were confident that Jesus would actually do so, for they knew how much He loved Lazarus and them.

JESUS DELAYS HIS RETURN

They sent out their cry for help, but we read in John 11:6, "When [Jesus] heard that Lazarus was sick, he stayed where he was two more days." He loved them, but He didn't come to their rescue. Why? I can see Martha and Mary waiting by the side of their sick brother, expecting Jesus to walk through the door any minute. They knew He could have been there shortly, but as hour by hour passed, Jesus didn't show up. And Lazarus got worse and worse, and they watched him die.

Do you think they wondered during that time if Jesus really loved them? Don't you imagine they must have felt abandoned and forsaken by Jesus, knowing that He could have come and healed their brother but chose not to? Have you felt that way? I think we all go through similar reactions when there are no answers or the answers are delayed.

When Jesus finally arrived, it was too late; Lazarus was already dead. Martha was upset with Jesus. We read in verse 21 that she said to him, "Lord, . . . if you had been here, my brother would not have died." She asked Him for an answer to her question: *Why didn't you come, Lord?*

JESUS IS THE RESURRECTION AND THE LIFE

I find Jesus' words to her at this time very interesting. He did not defend His actions; He did not say, "Martha, let Me explain to you exactly what I did and why." No, when Martha was looking for answers to her unanswered questions, Jesus took her back to the basics.

Jesus said to her, "I am the resurrection and the life. He who believes in me will live, even though he dies; and whoever lives and believes in me will never die. Do you believe this?" (vv. 25–26). He confronted Martha with the reality of who He was and caused her to change her thinking.

Instead of looking at the impossibilities and focusing on the unanswered questions, Jesus wanted her to think about who He was and what kind of power He had. And she confessed out loud, "Yes, Lord,

. . . I believe that you are the Christ, the Son of God, who was to come into the world" (v. 27).

When you don't have answers, stop and ask a different question: *Who do I believe Jesus is?* And then confess out loud exactly what you believe about the person of Jesus. It's important that you say it out loud, I think, so that you can hear your own confession of faith.

We may never know some of the answers we're looking for this side of heaven, but we can always confidently know the answer to the question, Who do I think Jesus is? By concentrating your thoughts on who He is, you will have the peace and strength you need for those unanswered questions. You will be able to soar on the winds of the storm and fly above it. If that was the question Jesus asked Martha when she wanted answers, then surely it is the starting place for us today when we want answers.

GOD'S TIMETABLE IS DIFFERENT FROM OURS

We all remember the end of this story; Jesus met their need by performing an incredible miracle and raising Lazarus from the dead. In this case, Mary and Martha finally got answers, as they saw their brother come forth after four days in the tomb. And that miracle was the talk of the town for days and weeks, as you can imagine. As a matter of fact, many people believed on Jesus when they heard about Lazarus and saw him alive (v. 45).

So eventually Martha and Mary could say to each other, "When it looked as though Jesus had forsaken us, He really was working on our behalf to do something even greater than we could imagine."

Sometimes it works out like that. We go through the no-answer period, the circumstances which make no sense to us whatsoever, but at a later date, in God's time, we are able to see what God's good purpose was.

Maybe some of you are now in that tough place where Mary and Martha were initially. You're wondering why Jesus hasn't come to you; you're feeling unloved and neglected by Him. Please do take courage and remember that often we misunderstand God's timetable. It may be that you will soon see the deliverance of God and your eyes will be opened to understand the whys.

WHEN THE ANSWER NEVER COMES

But what about those of you who don't get those answers? Your Lazarus never comes out of the tomb. You're left to face unanswered questions for the rest of your life. I'm sure many of you are in the midst of some situation for which you can find no answers. It is a storm that has no meaning, and God is silent. The heavens are like stone. You've begged for explanations, but none have come. What do you do when there are no answers?

Christians who have truly placed their faith in Jesus—who know His power and believe with all their hearts that He can rescue them from any circumstance—find it extremely difficult to face the fact that God is not going to answer their questions and that they will never know why certain things have happened. After all, we're supposed to have answers, aren't we? We've always told people that Jesus is the answer, that Jesus can meet all their needs. Therefore, those unanswered questions can undermine our faith and cause us to doubt the God we serve.

Well, I'm certainly not going to tell you that I have answers to your unanswered questions. I don't, and there are times when I throw up my hands and say, "I don't understand it."

In our family there is an unanswered question. My mother, now eighty-eight, is in a nursing home, and her mind is failing her. All her life my mother loved and read and studied the Word of God. It was truly her bread of life. Her greatest joy was to teach her Sunday class of women, and she invested hours each week into preparing her lessons.

I've never known anyone who loved the Bible as my mother did. She memorized great portions of it, and we have about ten Bibles she completely wore out because she turned those pages so often. These are family treasures we will distribute as keepsakes when she goes on to heaven.

I used to say that I knew my mother's mind would never fail her because she had so filled it with God's Word, and that would keep her mind strong. I believed that with all my heart. Now, as I see that she can't remember what she had for breakfast, or with whom she talked an hour ago, or even where she is or that her husband is now dead, I frequently wonder why God has allowed this to happen to her.

The end of her life is totally incongruous—to my mind—to what

it should be. I could understand a failing body, but I'm having difficulty understanding that her mind is failing her. At times I'm angry
about it, and I'm continually sad because of it. I talk it over with my
brothers and my friends, and none of us have answers. We shake our
heads in dismay and try to comfort each other with the truth that
God is still just and is still good. We believe it, but it doesn't answer our
questions.

EXPRESS YOUR FEELINGS

But how do we deal with it? Well, I think the Psalms are of great
help to us here, for frequently the psalmists expressed their frustration at the lack of answers.

In Psalm 44 the psalmist says to the Lord,

> *But now you have rejected and humbled us. . . .*
> *You have made us a reproach to our neighbors. . . .*
> *You have made us a byword among the nations. . . .*
> *All this happened to us,*
> > *though we had not forgotten you*
> > *or been false to your covenant. . . .*
> *Awake, O Lord! Why do you sleep? . . .*
> *Why do you hide your face*
> > *and forget our misery and oppression?*
> > > *—Psalm 44:9, 13–14, 17, 23–24*

That's an angry person expressing his anger openly to God. At
that moment, with no answers to his questions, he vented his anger toward God.

I want to say to you who have unanswered questions that anger and
frustration are normal. God is not going to condemn you for asking
the questions, for feeling anger at the unjust circumstances. He even
understands that you're likely to go through a period of being angry
at Him. God is big enough to handle your anger.

I don't want to imply that I think we should yell and scream at God when we please. But I do want to say to those of you who are living with difficult, unanswered questions that it's OK for you to tell God exactly how you feel about them. Please tell God; He knows your feelings and thoughts anyway, and if you don't ventilate those thoughts, or if you try to deny or ignore them, they will turn into bitterness and depression.

Who better to tell than God? He understands you completely, and no one will be fairer or gentler to you than He. He didn't chide Martha for her questions. He didn't zap the psalmists for voicing their anger. And isn't it interesting that all of that is recorded in Scripture for us to read. That's not an accident, you know; it's there to show us how to deal with unanswered questions. So, if the questions and the anger are smoldering inside of you, get alone with God and voice them to Him, out loud.

I notice that every time the psalmists voiced their frustration about the unanswered questions, soon they were led back to a basic trust in God that was the cornerstone of their lives. A frequent phrase you will find in the Psalms is "Why are you downcast, O my soul? Why so disturbed within me? Put your hope in God, for I will yet praise him, my Savior and my God" (Psalm 43:5).

You notice that the psalmist talked to himself. It's as though he sat down in a chair and said, "OK, let's have a talk. Why are you questioning God? Don't you know He's the One who can deliver you?"

Asaph expressed his rage at God: "Will the Lord reject us forever? Will he never show his favor again? Has his unfailing love vanished forever? Has his promise failed for all time? Has God forgotten to be merciful? Has he in anger withheld his compassion?" (Psalm 77:7–9).

REFOCUS YOUR MIND

Then, after saying those words of doubt and anger—and I think hearing in his own ears how foolish they were—Asaph said, "Then I thought, 'To this I will appeal: the years of the right hand of the Most High.' I will remember the deeds of the LORD; yes, I will remember your miracles of long ago. I will meditate on all your works and consider all your mighty deeds" (Psalm 77:10–12).

Asaph got the foolish, angry words out of his mouth, expressing to an understanding and patient God all his anger and frustration. And then he changed his thinking and started remembering all that God had done.

Ah, there's our answer, friends: renewing our minds with correct thinking about who God is and what He has done for us. Just as Martha needed to go back to the basics about Jesus, just as the psalmists needed to get back to who Jehovah God was and what He had done, so must we.

When the questions have no answers, we have to abandon them and be willing to live with the unanswered questions. But we don't have to live in despair or anger; the same God who, for whatever reason, does not answer our questions is the God who will bring us comfort and strength to face them.

TRUST THE LORD'S HEART

I often think of the question Jesus asked His disciples when many of His followers were forsaking Him. He said to the Twelve, "You do not want to leave too, do you?" Simon Peter answered, "Lord, to whom shall we go? You have the words of eternal life" (John 6:67–68).

Friends, where else will you go with your unanswered questions? If there are no answers from God, then trust Him to see you through. When you can't see why He's doing what He's doing, you can still trust His goodness and His love for you.

You may know the story of the hymn writer, Horatio Spafford. He was a wealthy Christian businessman living in Chicago in the nineteenth century. After the great Chicago fire of 1871, he was financially ruined. One summer he sent his wife and four daughters on ahead of him to London by ship, where he planned to join them in a few weeks. But the ship was in a collision with another ship, and all four of his daughters died. His wife, Anna, survived and sent him the now famous telegram, "Saved alone." Several weeks later, as Spafford's own ship passed the spot where his daughters died, at this horrible point in his life, when there were no answers, he wrote:

> *When peace, like a river, attendeth my way,*
> *When sorrows like sea billows roll;*
> *Whatever my lot, Thou hast taught me to say,*
> *"It is well, it is well with my soul."*

And, Lord, haste the day when the faith shall be sight,
The clouds be rolled back as a scroll,
The trump shall resound and the Lord shall descend,
"Even so"—it is well with my soul.

Could it be that those words were penned by Mr. Spafford to bring comfort to you in the midst of your storm even today? Someday our faith will turn to sight, either here or on heaven's shore. Meanwhile sing those words as you soar above the storm and know that the God of all creation will never take His eyes off of you and that His ear is always attentive to your cry.

CHAPTER 9

THE EAGLE'S RENEWAL

I remember a friend saying to me, "You know, I have all of the symptoms of a midlife crisis, and it just makes me so mad! I never thought this could happen to me!"

I can understand his feelings. It's dismaying to have to acknowledge that you are at midlife at all and, worse, are the victim of a malady you had always considered frivolous and childish! But midlife crises are real for many people. Whether at midlife or some other stage in our lives, all of us experience dismal, discouraging times when life no longer seems worth living. The eagle has a similar experience.

THE EAGLE'S MIDLIFE CRISIS

One of the most interesting characteristics about eagles is the molting process they go through. At about midlife, eagles experience an unusual chemical change in their bodies, and the time of molting begins. The eagle will seek out a secluded valley and sit there hour after hour with her head down. Her eyes are dry; her tear ducts are stopped. And one by one she starts to lose her feathers.

She no longer hunts for her food. Her talons become brittle from digging in the dirt for insects. She loses weight; death seems to be knocking at her door. Hope is dead. Her strength is gone. She has neither the inclination nor the energy to soar again.

In this dejected state, the eagle is very alone and isolated. It is a self-inflicted isolation, because she has left the comfort and safety of her nest, her community of eagles, and her mate. She is in a valley, not seated in her lofty nest. Her wings are drooping and sad, no longer catching the winds and soaring above the clouds. She doesn't look or feel or act like an eagle.

Suddenly she hears familiar sounds above her. Slowly she raises her head as the sounds get louder. It is the sound of her fellow eagles, flying above her in a circle formation.

She must wonder at first if they are mocking her, but then she realizes they are there to help. They keep flying above her, dropping tidbits of food into the valley for their molting, discouraged, ready-to-quit co-eagle. This continues as long as necessary, and, gradually, as the dejected eagle eats the food, her strength is renewed. She's able to soar again.

ELIJAH

Can you not picture yourself like that molting eagle, sitting in some isolated spot, feeling very alone, no longer acting or feeling like a Christian, perhaps even doubting that you ever were? After all, a Christian should never be discouraged or depressed—right? A Christian should always "have it together," whatever that means—right? A Christian should always have the desire and the ability to soar—right?

Wrong! Take a look at one stalwart of our faith, the prophet Elijah.

VICTORY

Mention Elijah and any Bible-knowledgeable person thinks of his great victory on Mount Carmel. I've stood on that mount many times, looking over the great valley and land of Israel stretched out below and rereading the Elijah story from 1 Kings 18:16–46. What a scene that was, as Elijah called down fire from heaven and destroyed all the false prophets. With incredible boldness and courage and faith, he challenged the prophets of Baal and of Asherah, eight hundred fifty in all, to a spiritual duel.

Here was a prophet of the true God standing against all the false prophets and mocking their god, Baal. When Baal didn't send down fire from heaven, Elijah had a little fun with the prophets: "'Shout louder!' he said. 'Surely he is a god! Perhaps he is deep in thought, or busy, or traveling. Maybe he is sleeping and must be awakened'" (1 Kings 18:27).

My, Elijah, what great courage you have! And faith! Wouldn't you love to have faith like that! He believed God would demonstrate His power, sending down fire and consuming a very wet sacrifice, demonstrating to all the people that the God of Israel is God alone. And then Elijah had all those false prophets slaughtered in the Kishon Valley. This was a mind-blowing example of a great man of God who demonstrated unwavering faith and courage.

DEJECTION

So how was it that in the very next chapter, the very next *day*, he became afraid and ran for his life? How could this same Elijah say, "'I have had enough, LORD,' he said. 'Take my life; I am no better than my ancestors'" (1 Kings 19:4).

He actually prayed that he might die. Is not Elijah a perfect example of an eagle who used to soar and is now in crisis mode, alone and dejected, frightened and disheartened, and ready to die?

After his great spiritual victory, one little woman scared him to death because she threatened to kill him.

> Now Ahab told Jezebel everything Elijah had done and how he had killed all the prophets with the sword. So Jezebel sent a messenger to Elijah to say, "May the gods deal with me, be it ever so severely, if by this time tomorrow I do not make your life like that of one of them." (1 Kings 19:1–2)

After what Elijah had just witnessed, knowing the power of his God to kill four hundred fifty false prophets, you would think he would say to Jezebel's messenger, "Does she think I am afraid of her? Does she not know what my God did on Mount Carmel? Is she not in fear of what He will do to her? You go tell Jezebel that I'm ready to face her down any time she wants. God is on my side, and I have no doubt that He will deliver me today just like He did yesterday."

That sounds like what a good Christian ought to say. It seems appropriate for this great man of God. It would look good on the six o'clock news!

Instead, we find this great prophet of God sitting in a valley, his feathers falling out, life draining out of his body, wishing he would die. Why, Elijah? What has caused this incredible shift from victory to despair?

THE CAUSES OF DISCOURAGEMENT

Elijah was discouraged because of exhaustion. It is not unusual to experience an almost immediate change like this when you have just experienced a great spiritual victory or had a mountaintop experience with God, as Elijah did. Some of this exhaustion is the physical result of the chemical change that takes place in your body as you go from an adrenaline high to an adrenaline low. Some of this exhaustion is the emotional letdown that comes with the realization that you're no longer on the mountaintop but back in real life, and the excitement of the experience is now a memory rather than a current event. You're physically and mentally worn out.

I find that I am often discouraged right after spiritual victories. In fact, I've come to expect it and call it my "Elijah syndrome." When I can see it coming, I try to be prepared for it, rather than surprised by it. I try to position my schedule and activities to allow for that droopy time of discouragement and defeat. But, of course, I'm not always keeping this in mind, and certainly it can catch me off guard. Then it is more difficult to recognize what's going on and respond to it appropriately.

LEARNING TO SOAR AGAIN

The challenge we now face as we find ourselves in that valley of discouragement and despair is how do we work our way out of it? Where do we find the motivation and the energy to soar again?

WE NEED HELP FROM THE BODY OF CHRIST

Did you notice that the eagle needs help from others? She needs that caring community of fellow eagles who come to her aid. Instead of squawking at her, or abandoning her, or ridiculing her, those eagles send down nourishment. In order to do that, they have to find extra food or give up some of theirs. They have to take the time required to find her and fly to her. They have to spread the word among the other eagles that one of their own needs help.

I love this characteristic of eagles, because it is such a beautiful picture of how the body of Christ should work. *Body of Christ* is a theological term we need to understand. It comes right from Scripture:

Just as each of us has one body with many members, and these members do not all have the same function, so in Christ we who are many form one body, and each member belongs to all the others. (Romans 12:4–5)

The body is a unit, though it is made up of many parts; and though all its parts are many, they form one body. So it is with Christ. For we were all baptized by one Spirit into one body—whether Jews or Greeks, slave or free—and we were all given the one Spirit to drink. (1 Corinthians 12:12–13)

Now you are the body of Christ, and each one of you is a part of it. (1 Corinthians 12:27)

From him [Jesus Christ] the whole body, joined and held together by every supporting ligament, grows and builds itself up in love, as each part does its work. (Ephesians 4:16)

We are all connected, regardless of our background, culture, race, gender, age, denomination, or social status. We who have been regenerated through faith in Jesus Christ and cleansed by His blood become a part of the body of Christ, and our responsibility is to build each other up. We ought to be circling above, dropping nourishment and encouragement to any fallen, discouraged, despairing fellow believer.

But all too often the Christian community condemns and accuses, gossips and criticizes, lectures and admonishes, rather than nourishes and encourages. It is one of the saddest commentaries on us as a body of believers because Jesus told us, "All men will know that you are my disciples, if you love one another" (John 13:35).

Please understand, I'm not advocating that Christians take a soft stand against wrongdoing or sin. When a brother or sister in Christ has strayed from the path, we are given clear guidance in Scripture on how to try to restore that person—and that includes a confrontation. We don't ignore or tolerate the sinning believer, for their sin can damage the cause of Christ and the testimony of His body. We know also that the sinning believer's best good will come through confession and restoration. But even that must be done in great love and compassion, with the understanding that we ourselves are just as vulnerable to sin.

I think of a friend who went through a very long "molting" period in her life. For reasons that no one—not even the woman herself—could understand, she became severely depressed and was totally ready to quit. Doctors could not find the right medication to help her; counseling did not reveal any hidden problems that needed to be dealt with. But, nonetheless, for over a year she sat in that valley of despondency, truly despairing of life.

Thank God for her many Christian friends, who simply were there for her through it all. Baffled as we all were by this molting experience, we just kept nourishing her. We called her, invited her to events, prayed for and with her, spent much time listening to and empathizing with her. It was not always easy, because the depression did not go away overnight. But we never gave up. We hovered overhead, like eagles do, like the body of Christ is meant to do, and through it, God brought deliverance.

How good it is to see her functioning again in ministry for the Lord with joy and enthusiasm. How blessed we all are to have her back again, encouraging us and contributing to the good of the body. I doubt that she could tell you even now that she knows why she went through this long period of molting, but she *can* tell you that her fellow Christian eagles were of great help in bringing her through.

Jesus always dealt gently with those who were disheartened and ready to give up, even if their problems were self-inflicted. His gentleness was evident in the way He dealt with the woman caught in adultery. First, He protected her from her accusers, and, once they were alone, He didn't say a lot to her. "Has no one condemned you?" He asked. Obviously they had not. "'Then neither do I condemn you,' Jesus declared. 'Go now and leave your life of sin'" (John 8:10–11).

Just as Jesus did not need to expound on her sin or lecture her about it, we don't usually need to remind the fallen Christian of just how awful his fall has been. The Holy Spirit within him will do a better job of that than we ever can. (If there is no obvious conviction of that sin, we have a right to question whether or not the person is truly connected with God through faith in Christ. A true believer will know conviction when he is in sin.) After the necessary confrontation, our approach should be one of restoration and love, giving nourishment and encouragement so that our brother or sister in Christ can truly soar again.

Ever think about how Jesus dealt with Peter after the Resurrection? Peter had dreadfully failed the Lord, but Jesus never said, "Peter, how could you have done what you did to Me? How could you have denied Me with cursings?" No, Jesus knew that Peter was a "walking wounded" at that moment, a person who undoubtedly felt he had made a fatal mistake from which he could never recover. And so Jesus just gently talked with him and asked, "Peter, do you love me?" (John 21:15–17).

Don't you think Jesus was saying to Peter, "I know you've failed Me, but if you truly love Me, we still have a future together"? Jesus understood that you can fail a person you love, as Peter had failed Him. Jesus wanted to restore Peter, not condemn him, so He brought loving ointment to Peter's wounds so that the scab could form and the healing take place. And it worked beautifully.

A pastor's wife friend of mine started a Sunday school class for single parents in their church. Although Astrid has never been in their shoes, she cared for them and helped them develop a family group where they could talk with and help each other. As I met with the group one Sunday, each of those single parents told me how much the class meant to them. My friend was God's eagle, circling overhead, helping this group of hurt and discouraged Christians, giving them nourishment and encouragement.

WE NEED PHYSICAL REST AND NOURISHMENT

In the midst of his flight and fear, running for his life from little ol' Jezebel, Elijah went into the desert alone, sat down under a broom tree, and got ready to die. But the angel of the Lord brought him a cake of bread and a jar of water. "He ate and drank and then lay down again" (1 Kings 19:6).

That may not seem like a "spiritual" solution, but it is often God's recipe for getting us soaring again. We need to sleep and eat and eat and sleep. We need to just do nothing and allow time for our bodies to be physically replenished and nourished.

In our busy, crowded lives, that becomes more and more difficult. We feel guilty if we stop. We are restless if we slow down and attend to our own needs for rest. I definitely speak to myself as I write this, because, as my friends will tell you, I'm not good at taking time "away." I have a list of good reasons, but part of it is that very soon I become restless and feel as if time is wasting when I simply stop for a while.

Like Elijah, we need times of rest, times away from our normal duties. Elijah's recovery from this down period was not overnight. It was a bit of a struggle for him. Even after weeks of being alone with God and being nourished by God, he was still despondent.

> He [Elijah] replied, "I have been very zealous for the Lord God Almighty. The Israelites have rejected your covenant, broken down your altars, and put your prophets to death with the sword. I am the only one left, and now they are trying to kill me too." (1 Kings 19:10)

Don't you think Elijah had succumbed to our human tendency toward self-pity? It seems to me he was in the midst of a major pity party. "Poor me," he said. "I've been a good guy for the Lord, and look where it has gotten me. I'm the only one left standing up for the Lord."

Well, not exactly, Elijah. Your facts are a little off. First, it was Baal's prophets who were put to death, not the Lord's. You are not the only one left in all Israel who believes in the true God. There are seven thousand in Israel who have not bowed down to Baal (1 Kings 19:18). And what evidence is there that your enemies are still trying to kill you? It has been a few weeks since you started running, and Jezebel said she was going to have your head in one day's time: "May the gods deal with me, be it ever so severely, if by this time tomorrow I do not make your life like that of one of them" (v. 2). Well, Elijah, you are not dead yet, and the time frame for her threat has long run out.

You see, in our pity parties we always exaggerate the negative and overlook the positive. Things always look much worse than they really are, as we wallow in self-pity. Yet self-pity is one of the most common cesspools for us as believers and one of the most difficult from which to extricate ourselves. Could it be that we actually enjoy the slime and mud of self-pity?

Note that while Elijah was in this valley of despair, even though God was dealing with him, nourishing him, and working in his life, Elijah did not snap his fingers and pull himself up to soar again quickly. In fact, the Lord at this time revealed himself to Elijah in a most marvelous way, and even that was not enough to snap him out of it.

The Lord told him, "Go out and stand on the mountain in the presence of the LORD, for the LORD is about to pass by" (v. 11). Elijah did that, and God revealed Himself to Elijah in that still, small voice. I've sung and directed the chorus in Mendelssohn's *Elijah* that deals with this incident, and it is one of the most moving moments in the entire oratorio. The Lord was not in the wind; the Lord was not in the earthquake; the Lord was not in the fire. But the Lord came to Elijah in a gentle whisper—a still voice.

Wow! Surely that would do it for Elijah! God had just demonstrated His care and concern through divine manipulation of the elements. What a display of God's power and love that must have been. Now you're ready to go again—right, Elijah?

Well, not exactly. Even with all this evidence of God's care and power, Elijah headed back to the cave. He was truly stuck in the valley of despair. How could he ever get out and become a powerful man of God again?

WE NEED TO OBEY GOD

Elijah's recovery began with simple obedience. After Elijah went back into the cave, God asked him again, "What are you doing here, Elijah?" Elijah gave the same answer he had before: "I am the only one left, and now they are trying to kill me too" (1 Kings 19:13–14).

Fear had taken over his mind; he was not making rational decisions. He still could not see his way out of the valley of despair.

Then the Lord told him, "Go back the way you came, and go to the Desert of Damascus" (v. 15). Rather strange instructions, don't you think? The Lord told Elijah to head right back to the place he was running from. All those days and weeks Elijah had been avoiding it, because that was where Jezebel threatened to kill him. He was trying to get away from Jezebel. But instead of sending him to a safer location, God sent him back to the place where his fear and despair had begun.

I've seen God work in the same way so often, in my own life and the lives of others. It seems to be a basic principle of the Christian life that God doesn't let us out of a difficult situation until we have found victory in that place.

I had a job once with what I described as an impossible boss. All I wanted to do was run away. I got my résumé together, interviewed several times, and a couple of positions looked more than promising. I was led to believe I was a shoo-in. But for various reasons beyond my control, each position fell through, and I was stuck in that job with the miserable boss.

I griped and complained and held a major pity party, until finally I heard God's still voice informing me that there was no way out of this until I was on the victory side. For two more years I worked there, but with a completely changed attitude and purpose. God changed my heart, and I was able to see that job as the place God had put me for as long as it was His pleasure. In retrospect, I now can see why that was His plan for me, and I praise Him for the good things He did in those two years.

Running away is never God's way of dealing with a problem. Sometimes He lets us out of difficult situations, but never until He has worked in us all that He wants to accomplish through it. You see, most of us don't learn God's principles too well until we are in the school of hard knocks.

So Elijah went back to the dreaded place—but on the way God sent an answer.

> So Elijah went from there and found Elisha son of Shaphat. He was plowing with twelve yoke of oxen, and he himself was driving the twelfth pair. Elijah went up to him and threw his cloak around him. Elisha then

left his oxen and ran after Elijah. "Let me kiss my father and mother good-bye," he said, "and then I will come with you."

"Go back," Elijah replied. "What have I done to you?"

So Elisha left him and went back. He took his yoke of oxen and slaughtered them. He burned the plowing equipment to cook the meat and gave it to the people, and they ate. Then he set out to follow Elijah and became his attendant. (1 Kings 19:19–21)

Sometimes the way we defeat discouragement is simply to obey. Even when we don't want to; even when our feelings aren't working right; even when everything in us wants to run away and hide, feel sorry for ourselves, and bail out. It came down to a sheer act of obedience for Elijah to go back the way he came. But when he did, Elijah found the encouragement God was preparing for him.

Keep in mind that we will be willing and able to obey in the face of discouragement only when we have instilled obedience as a way of life before we became discouraged. Elijah had made a commitment to obey the Lord, and that discipline, that practice of obeying, was a natural response for him. It would have been difficult if not impossible for Elijah to obey during his time of deep discouragement if he had not learned obedience earlier in his life.

WE NEED ELISHAS!

Elisha has a warm place in my heart. What a giving, loving man. When Elijah put his cloak around him, he recognized that as a call to serve Elijah. He abandoned everything, gave what he had to those around him, and ran off to follow Elijah and become his attendant.

Do you have an Elisha in your life? Are you someone else's Elisha? I thank God for a few people who have continually been there for me. My best friend, Fran, is a great gift from God to me. She is my cheerleader who never ceases to encourage and nourish me. Others have also been Elishas to me, and without them I probably would have found my own cave somewhere along the way and run away.

When you find yourself in that valley of despair, spend some time with a person who will encourage you, whose faith is strong. Overcome the tendency to isolate yourself; reach out to those who are there to help you. God gives us Elishas for that very purpose.

And then be ready to be that kind of person to your friends when they are going through discouraging times. We need to share our faith with each other during our days of discouragement. Someone else can have faith for you when you're finding it impossible to believe, and his faith will bolster and encourage you.

Hebrews 10:25 says: "Let us not give up meeting together, as some are in the habit of doing, but let us encourage one another—and all the more as you see the Day approaching."

OUR STRENGTH IS RENEWABLE

When you're in the valley of despair, with your eagle's wings drooping and lifeless, you often feel that life will never be good again, that you'll never again know joy or laughter or lightness of spirit. But I want to encourage you, if that is where you are right now, to know without a doubt that there is life abundant waiting for you. Don't forget God's power and His promises. Isaiah reminds us:

> *He has sent me to bind up the brokenhearted,*
> *to proclaim freedom for the captives*
> *and release from darkness for the prisoners . . .*
> *to comfort all who mourn,*
> *and provide for those who grieve in Zion—*
> *to bestow on them a crown of beauty*
> *instead of ashes,*
> *the oil of gladness*
> *instead of mourning,*
> *and a garment of praise*
> *instead of a spirit of despair.*
> *—Isaiah 61:1–3*

Having watched a dream die in my own life almost twenty years ago, I went through an eighteen-month recovery period. My eagle's wings were definitely not working well, and I thought life would never be good again. I was prepared for a dreary and unfulfilled existence.

But I began to obey God, spend time in His Word, fellowship with believers who nourished me and bolstered my faith, and reach out to others with love and concern. And God brought me back to soar again as I had never soared before.

I journaled my way back through this period of time, and that journal now is a reminder of God's care for me during my "molting" stage. As He did Elijah, so He fed me and sent Elishas my way; and little by little, my strength was renewed.

Let me share one entry from my journal, made eighteen months or so after this journey back from a broken dream began. After I had let go of my dream, embraced the pain instead of trying to run from it, avoided the temptation to give up, and began to find healing by becoming involved in helping others, joy and happiness and fulfillment and hope began to reenter my life. Here's what I wrote at that point:

> Lord, You've made a garden out of my wilderness and my desert. Only You could do that. Jesus is all the world to me—may it ever be increasingly so! May I never turn again to my folly!

And now, over the past almost twenty years since I made that entry, God has brought me to new places. He has done a new thing for me, and I am glad. There are still hills to climb and obstacles to overcome. It has not been a "storybook" ending, but it has been better than the "happily-ever-afters" of the fairy tales. What God is doing in my life is to use that painful experience to make me more like Jesus, to help transform me into His likeness with ever-increasing glory. I want to tell you, that is exciting. And He has even used my sorrow and my pain to bring glory to Him, allowing me to reach others I would never be able to otherwise.

Here's a passage to hold on to in your molting period:

> *Praise the LORD, O my soul;*
> *all my inmost being, praise his holy name.*
> *Praise the LORD, O my soul,*
> *and forget not all his benefits—*

who forgives all your sins
   and heals all your diseases,
who redeems your life from the pit
   and crowns you with love and compassion,
who satisfies your desires with good things
   so that your youth is renewed like the eagle's.

—*Psalm 103:1–5*

God gave us this wonderful real-life picture of renewal in the eagle, created just that way so that we can believe our strength can be renewed. If God can do it for eagles, if He desires to renew eagles, then surely we can believe that He can and will renew us as well.

I am continually comforted by the knowledge that God knows and understands me in my weakest moments as well as in my best ones.

As a father has compassion on his children,
   so the Lord has compassion on those who fear him;
for he knows how we are formed,
   he remembers that we are dust.

—*Psalm 103:13–14*

Even youths grow tired and weary,
   and young men stumble and fall;
but those who hope in the Lord
   will renew their strength.
They will soar on wings like eagles;
   they will run and not grow weary,
   they will walk and not be faint.

—*Isaiah 40:30–31*

SOAR BEFORE YOU RUN AND WALK

Notice that when our strength is renewed like the eagle, first we mount up on wings. Then we run, and then we walk. Does that sound a little backwards to you? Aren't you supposed to crawl before you walk and walk before you run?

In this renewal process, where we are learning again to soar and are in the renewal process, we need to get our wings back first. We need to soar in those heavenly places and get God's perspective. We need to remember who we are in Christ and whose we are because of Christ. Once we're soaring again, we're ready to run the race set before us. Then we have the desire and the power to walk this lonely road down here.

It's good to remember that this world is not a friend to God and that as God's children we are living as aliens and strangers in an unfriendly world. That's where we walk every day; that's where we run the race every day. Running and walking take a lot of grace and power and love and patience and compassion. Those are the attributes of God our Father, and we can only demonstrate them in this sin-filled world if we truly have soared like an eagle and been filled with the presence and Spirit of God.

So the soaring has to come before the running and the walking. Yes, it's a little backwards to our minds, but then God's ways usually are different from ours—have you noticed? If you're in need of renewal, seek first to soar before trying to run your race.

Seek ye first the kingdom of God, and His righteousness; and all these things shall be added unto you. (Matthew 6:33 KJV)

Since, then, you have been raised with Christ, set your hearts on things above, where Christ is seated at the right hand of God. Set your minds on things above, not on earthly things. (Colossians 3:1–2)

Get your heart and mind soaring in the heavenly realms, and then you will be renewed to do your running and walking.

IT'S ALL ABOUT GOD!

The story of Job has fascinated us through the ages. To see all he went through, all he lost, all he suffered, and realize that he never turned his back on God. He never cursed God, as his wife suggested he do. "Shall we accept good from God, and not trouble?" was his response (Job 2:10). And we shake our heads in admiration and wonder at how one man could hold up so well under such terrible loss.

Toward the end of the book, after Job's friends have given their feckless advice, the Lord speaks to Job. It's quite a lecture, found in Job 39–41. Much of God's message to Job was focused on reminding Job who God is.

During this memory lesson, God said to Job:

"Does the eagle soar at your command
and build his nest on high?

He dwells on a cliff and stays there at night;
*   a rocky crag is his stronghold.*
From there he seeks out his food;
*   his eyes detect it from afar.*
His young ones feast on blood,
*   and where the slain are, there is he."*
                              —*Job 39:27–30*

God used the eagle, along with others of His creation, to teach Job a lesson about God. He reiterated some of the characteristics of the eagle, pointing out his unique abilities and attributes. In essence, he was asking Job, "Did you create such a creature as this? Could you? No, Job, the eagle is another evidence of My majesty, My sovereignty, My power, and My creativity. Job, what I want you to know is that this life is not all about you; it's all about Me!"

A PARADIGM SHIFT

Each of us sees the world through his own individual paradigm. We don't often see things as they are, but as *we* are, and as we have been conditioned to see them.

You and I have many paradigms in our heads on which we base our values and our behavior. We interpret everything through our own personal paradigms. We are convinced they are correct; we *assume* they are correct; we seldom question whether or not they are correct. We will defend our paradigms quickly because we think we are right.

For example, what are some common paradigms about heaven and how to get there?

Paradigm #1: All roads lead to God as long as you are sincere.
Paradigm #2: Do the best you can and God will let you into heaven.
Paradigm #3: As long as your good deeds outnumber your bad deeds, you'll get to heaven.
Paradigm #4: Go to church every Sunday and be a good person and you'll get to heaven.
Paradigm #5: There is no heaven or God.

In order to become a true child of God, a person must have a total paradigm shift from those wrong perceptions. There has to come that moment when a person says, "Oh, I see!" and he or she recognizes the true paradigm as given in the Bible: "Jesus answered, 'I am the way and the truth and the life. No one comes to the Father except through me'" (John 14:6).

THE CORRECT PARADIGM IS ALL-IMPORTANT

You can see how absolutely critical it is that we are looking at life through the correct paradigm. If your paradigms are incorrect, if you are deceived in some way in how you view things, you may be very sincere, but you will be very sincerely wrong!

This is a very simple truth, but seldom do we think about it: When you are deceived, you don't know it. The nature of deception lies in our inability to perceive that we are deceived. So, with wrong paradigms, we can live our lives in tragic deception and never know it.

SELF-CENTERED PARADIGMS

Self-centeredness has been with us since the beginning of time, but never has it been so popularized as in the last few decades. Our society has legitimized it, even honored it. You see it in everything from our advertising slogans, to our school curriculums, to our political philosophies, to our legislation.

Here are some recognizable examples of the self-centered paradigms that are very readily accepted by most people in today's culture:

- You only go around once, so go for the gusto.
- You deserve a break today.
- Truth is relative; whatever works for you is your truth.
- Do what feels good.
- A woman has a right to destroy a baby within her body.
- Any sexual orientation is acceptable.
- You must have good self-esteem.
- Character is not an issue when it comes to leadership.
- God is in all of us.

As a result of these erroneous paradigms through which most people in our society view the world and establish their values, we have seen an erosion in the morals of our society, an increase in crime, a disintegration of marriages and families, an abandonment of truth and truth-telling, and an acceptance of perversion. That is how the apostle Paul described it in his letter to Timothy:

> There will be terrible times in the last days. People will be lovers of themselves, lovers of money, boastful, proud, abusive, disobedient to their parents, ungrateful, unholy, without love, unforgiving, slanderous, without self-control, brutal, not lovers of the good, treacherous, rash, conceited, lovers of pleasure rather than lovers of God—having a form of godliness but denying its power. (2 Timothy 3:1–5)

This is what happens to a society and a world that abandons the right paradigm—the God-given worldview—and shifts to the wrong one.

PARADIGM SHIFT: IT'S ALL ABOUT GOD!

The Bible presents an entirely different paradigm that not many ever truly embrace. As God said to Job, "Does the eagle soar at your command," so He would say to us, "Do you think that life is all about you—your desires, your fulfillment, your happiness, your dreams and goals, your rights? Please, think again! It's not all about you—it's all about God!"

This paradigm is not in sync with worldly views, not even in sync with some evangelical Christian views. It will cause you to push the envelope and think in very different ways. This will not always be comfortable. It will take time and practice. But I assure you that with this paradigm shift, there is great joy and freedom in store for you.

Everything is about God, not about us. Consider what we learn from Scripture.

CREATION IS ALL ABOUT GOD

Everything created, including you, was created for God's purposes. Colossians 1:16 says: "For by him all things were created: things in heaven and on earth, visible and invisible, whether thrones or powers or rulers or authorities; all things were created by him and for him."

THE GOSPEL IS ALL ABOUT GOD

In our self-centeredness, we can start to think that the gospel—the good news that Jesus came to earth, born of a virgin, and died on the cross to pay the penalty for our sins—is all about us. Consider these passages:

> But you are a chosen people, a royal priesthood, a holy nation, a people belonging to God, that you may declare the praises of him who called you out of darkness into his wonderful light. (1 Peter 2:9)

> And God raised us up with Christ and seated us with him in the heavenly realms in Christ Jesus, in order that in the coming ages he might show the incomparable riches of his grace, expressed in his kindness to us in Christ Jesus. (Ephesians 2:6–7)

> Who [God] has saved us and called us to a holy life—not because of anything we have done but because of his own purpose and grace. (2 Timothy 1:9)

If we have the wrong paradigm, we will trace the gospel back to God's need for us instead of tracing it back to the sovereign grace that rescues sinners who need God.

In spite of the fact that God was in no way obligated to save us, He chose to provide a way of salvation for us, so that He would be praised. Through the salvation He offers us, the glory of His grace can be manifest to the world. Because we are born into His family and become His chosen people, we are then able to declare His praises.

That is what salvation is all about—it's all about bringing praise and glory to the God who provided it, even though He didn't have to and we don't deserve it!

PRAYER IS ALL ABOUT GOD

Praying is about bringing glory to God. Everything we pray should be prayed for the purpose that God's name will be glorified. That's what it means to pray "in the name of Jesus."

Therefore, when you pray for forgiveness of your sins, it is so that through that forgiveness, God will be honored. When you pray for salvation for others, it is for the purpose of glorifying God through their salvation. When you pray that your needs will be met, it is so that God can be praised through the meeting of your needs. When you pray that your health will improve, it is for the purpose of bringing praise to the name of Jesus.

That paradigm changes your prayer life. It makes you realize how much of your praying has been self-centered. It causes you to think, *Why am I asking God to heal me? Because I don't want to be sick? Because I hate pain? Because I don't like to be uncomfortable?* That is self-centered praying; it's all about you. But when your prayers are all about God, they change and become more like this:

"Lord, if Your name can be glorified through my healing, then I ask You to heal me."

"Lord, if it will bring praise and glory to You by meeting my financial need, I ask You to meet this need."

"Lord, please forgive my sins so that Your name may be praised for forgiving my sins."

THE CHRISTIAN LIFE IS ALL ABOUT GOD

Our daily living is not about our finding fulfillment or realizing our dreams or finding relief from pain and struggles. It is not about how we can amass success or money, or what we can do to feel good about ourselves.

The Christian life is all about God. Jesus prayed: "Now this is eternal life: that they may know you, the only true God, and Jesus Christ, whom you have sent" (John 17:3).

In our society, we look through the paradigm of materialism and success. We judge people by the things they accumulate, the awards they win, the rung of ladder to which they have climbed. Even in our evangelical world, we often see our lives through this worldly paradigm. It's the biggest churches, the best musicians, the highest numbers we tend to honor. If the crowds don't come, if the seats aren't filled, if people are not sufficiently entertained and amused, we hold those programs in low esteem.

We need a paradigm shift away from the materialism- and entertainment-based society in which we live to seeing our lives as being all about God and what brings glory to His name.

Let me see if I can illustrate this for you so that in your everyday life you can see what a difference it makes when you see your life through this paradigm: It's all about God!

SCENARIO #1:

You're having a bad day. Your co-worker has hurt your feelings. She is very insensitive to you. She just gave you another one of her lectures—about how you need to do the job differently. She thinks she's your boss, and you're just sick and tired of the way she treats you. Every day it's "Do this, do that." Who needs it? Who appointed her your manager?

At this point, with this attitude, you are looking at your problem with your co-worker through the paradigm of your rights and your feelings. Is that making you happy? No, it is causing you stress and making you angry. Who's winning? Not you, that's for sure.

The reason is, you've got the wrong paradigm. Suppose you choose to see this person through this new paradigm: It's all about God! What does that mean and how does that change anything?

It means that this personal struggle you are having with your co-worker is not all about your feelings or your rights, because everything in your life is all about God. The apostle Paul said, "Accept one another, then, just as Christ accepted you, in order to bring praise to God" (Romans 15:7). This new paradigm will allow you to accept your co-worker as Christ has accepted you, in order to bring praise to God. It's not all about you; it's all about God!

It's a new way to see the people who treat you wrongly, unkindly, inappropriately. They are not in your life by accident. God has a purpose for giving you that co-worker, that job, that boss, that mate, that child, that sibling, that friend. It's all about God and His purposes for your life.

If you decide to accept your co-worker and let God be praised through your relationship with her, that will affect your response to this co-worker. It doesn't mean you will become a doormat. It doesn't mean you will jump every time the co-worker hollers. But it does mean that your co-worker's behavior toward you will no longer irritate you like it did. It means that you can learn to let it roll off of you without getting your feelings hurt. It means you can have peace in the midst of that unpleasant situation. Now, I ask you, who wins?

Scenario #2:

You come from a very dysfunctional family. Your parents never showed any of their children love or affection. There was a lot of fighting in your home. Your father was drunk quite often. It was hell on earth, and, as a result, you just can't ever feel good about yourself. You feel as though your parents really ruined your life. Your self-image is warped, and your self-esteem is very low because of this dysfunctional childhood.

As long as you see your past through your pain and loss, you will never be able to put it behind you and move forward. But when you choose to look at your past through this new paradigm—It's all about God!—you have a completely new way of dealing with those past hurts.

Once you understand that even your past is all about God, your past can be used by God to bring glory to His name. Remember what Joseph said to his brothers, who had greatly abused him? He was from a dysfunctional family, too, but God used him mightily. And he said to those same brothers: "You intended to harm me, but God intended it for good to accomplish what is now being done, the saving of many lives" (Genesis 50:20).

Paul wrote to the Philippians: "Brothers, I do not consider myself yet to have taken hold of it. But one thing I do: Forgetting what is behind and straining toward what is ahead, I press on toward the goal to win the prize for which God has called me heavenward in Christ Jesus" (Philippians 3:13–14).

That doesn't mean that God wanted you to have an abusive, un-happy childhood. No, that came as a result of sin in this sin-cursed world. But God can heal those wounds and give you a new hope so that you can go forward to the good things He has planned for you. However, you have to look at your past through this new paradigm: It's all about God!

If you choose to do that, the pain of your past will gradually subside. You will discover that your self-esteem issue goes away, because life is not about your feeling good about yourself; it's about God and bringing glory to Him in any way possible—even through your painful past.

SCENARIO #3:

You're a very successful woman. You are always rushed and busy with your high-powered job. You've broken through the glass ceiling. You're a lawyer, and they're going to be making decisions about new partnerships soon. You intend to become a partner in this law firm; you've been working night and day for this promotion. So you get there early and stay late and turn in lots of billable hours. The bosses are pretty impressed with you, and you're pretty sure you're going to make partner this year.

Life is turning out the way you planned it. All that hard work and education is going to finally pay off. Your goals and plans are within your grasp. And with your success will come money, fancy offices, respect, lots of perks. True, you are a believer in Jesus Christ, and you love the Lord, but there's no question that your job has your first loyalty.

Looking at your job through that paradigm is a recipe for disappointment and heartbreak. That job will not live up to your expectations. Even if you achieve the success you have planned, you will discover the emptiness that is at the top. And you will be ever struggling to find that position, that next level, which will fulfill its promise of satisfaction and happiness.

If you will choose to see your career through this new paradigm—It's all about God!—your attitude will turn around dramatically. That doesn't mean that you would not or should not aspire to become a partner. It doesn't preclude you from climbing the ladder to business success. But you will recognize the opportunity that God is giving you to demonstrate His glory in your workplace through your efforts, even through your success.

It helps you to remember that you are a steward of the talents, abilities, and opportunities that God allows to come your way. They are given to you by God for a period of time so that you can use them to bring honor to Him. We need people in all levels of the business world who are there to demonstrate God's power and glory through their work. You will still do good work, but the motivation will be different. You will actually begin to experience the principle Paul taught the Colossians: "Whatever you do, whether in word or deed, do it all in the name of the Lord Jesus, giving thanks to God the Father through him" (Colossians 3:17).

Doing it all "in the name of the Lord Jesus" means that we do it in order to bring glory to His name. With that paradigm shift, you realize that your job and your success are not all about you; they are all about God!

WHAT IS YOUR GREATEST STRUGGLE RIGHT NOW?

What is the most difficult situation in your life at the present time? It could be a circumstance, like finances or health; it could be a relationship; it could be an inward struggle you are having about your own self-worth; it could be a feeling of despair or depression. If you had to name your greatest struggle at the present time, what would it be?

Would you be willing to see that situation through this new paradigm: "I have been crucified with Christ and I no longer live, but Christ lives in me. The life I live in the body, I live by faith in the Son of God, who loved me and gave himself for me" (Galatians 2:20).

The apostle Paul is telling us the same thing God was teaching Job when He reminded him of the power and grandeur and uniqueness of the eagle. Everything is all about God, not all about us, and when we finally get that new paradigm firmly planted in our wandering minds, it changes us forever.

WHAT DO YOU KNOW ABOUT GOD?

This paradigm shift might frighten you if you don't know what God is like. Obviously, this topic takes many more pages than we have now. But you find out what God is like by spending time in His Word. It tells us, to mention a few, that our God is

- all-powerful
- all-knowing
- all-wise
- sovereign
- everywhere present
- loving
- good
- patient
- gracious
- merciful

The Bible also describes in detail the Lord's loving care for His children. His holy character and His love for us are expressed in many passages of the Bible.

- He has good plans for you! "'For I know the plans I have for you,' declares the LORD, 'plans to prosper you and not to harm you, plans to give you hope and a future'" (Jeremiah 29:11).
- He delights in you! "The LORD your God is with you, he is mighty to save. He will take great delight in you, he will quiet you with his love, he will rejoice over you with singing" (Zephaniah 3:17).
- He will never leave you nor forsake you! "Keep your lives free from the love of money and be content with what you have, because God has said, 'Never will I leave you; never will I forsake you'" (Hebrews 13:5).
- Nothing can separate you from His love! "For I am convinced that neither death nor life, neither angels nor demons, neither the present nor the future, nor any powers, neither height nor depth, nor anything else in all creation, will be able to separate us from the love of God that is in Christ Jesus our Lord" (Romans 8:38–39).
- He never takes His eyes off of you, and He is always listening for your cry! "The eyes of the LORD are on the righteous and his ears are attentive to their cry" (Psalm 34:15).

THE RESULTS ARE
ALMOST TOO GOOD TO BE TRUE

So when you start to view everything in your life through this paradigm shift—"It's all about God!"—that will not frighten you if you know what God is like.

This will be true of the small, irritating things that happen in our daily lives:

- You're having a bad hair day.
- Murphy's Law is at work, and everything is going wrong.
- Someone said something unkind and untrue about you, and your feelings are hurt.
- Your boss didn't give you the recognition you deserve.
- Your mate forgot your birthday.

It will also be true of the larger and more serious things:

- You have discovered a lump in your breast.
- You're facing bankruptcy.
- Your spouse just walked out on you.
- Your biological clock is ticking, and you can't get pregnant.
- Prince Charming hasn't come along, and you're still single.
- An important relationship has been damaged.
- Your child is rebellious.
- Your parents are now needing constant care.

Everything that happens to us can be viewed through this new paradigm.

How you respond to the circumstances and situations of your life is transformed when you stop and say, "It's all about God!" All of your life is about God's working His will through you so that Jesus is glorified in you, by whatever means.

This paradigm takes you out of an earthly orbit and puts you into a heavenly orbit. This is wind beneath your wings, and you truly are soaring. It takes you up so high you can see the invisible things of this world, the really important things. "For our light and momentary troubles are achieving for us an eternal glory that far outweighs them all.

So we fix our eyes not on what is seen, but on what is unseen. For what is seen is temporary, but what is unseen is eternal" (2 Corinthians 4:17–18).

This paradigm shift will

- reduce your stress,
- give you joy,
- give your life purpose and meaning,
- free you from the approval of others,
- free you from the need for "good self-esteem,"
- free you from your past,
- make you content with who you are and where you are,
- turn bad experiences into productive ones, and
- improve your relationships,

just to mention a few.

BORN TO SOAR

When you live each day in the reality that your life and everything that happens to you are all about God, you're soaring like an eagle. Nothing can bring you down for long because you have learned the most basic, fundamental truth about the Christian life.

I am not a trained counselor, nor do I have the gift of counseling. But because I am in a leadership role with women, I frequently read and hear the sad stories of many women, and men too, for that matter. And almost without fail, each sad story is told to me from the viewpoint "It's all about me."

I've begun to take note of how directly despair is connected to this self-focused paradigm. If seeing everything as being all about us brought us great joy and fulfillment, it would be easier to understand why we are so easily addicted to it. But just the opposite is true.

Jesus taught this life-changing paradigm shift when He was here on earth: "Whoever finds his life will lose it, and whoever loses his life for my sake will find it" (Matthew 10:39).

The twelve men closest to Him were befuddled by such a paradoxical statement, and few of us today who call ourselves disciples of Jesus Christ have done better. It is so natural for us to see everything through our own paradigm and so difficult for us to see our lives through God's paradigm.

Let me assure you, it can be done. Soaring like an eagle is losing your life to find it. And it is absolutely possible for all true disciples. But it is done daily, sometimes hourly. It is an intentional and practiced lifestyle, a paradigm shift we choose to embrace, often against our logic and our emotions.

Though I am fully aware that I do not soar every day in every situation, I truly don't want to settle for anything less. I trust you have been encouraged through these pages to join me in this pursuit. Let's "spur one another on toward love and good deeds" (Hebrews 10:24), as we soar above life's circumstances and get that wonderful eternal perspective which the high places offer. Then we experience that paradoxical truth that life is at its best when we remember that everything is all about God!

NOTES

CHAPTER 2: EAGLE EYES
1. Jim Elliot, The Journals of Jim Elliot, ed. Elisabeth Elliot (Old Tappan, N.J.: Revell, 1978), entry for October 28, 1949); see also Elisabeth Elliot, *Shadow of the Almighty: The Life and Testament of Jim Elliot* (New York: Harper, 1958), 46.

CHAPTER 3: EAGLE FLYING LESSONS
1. Elisabeth Elliot, *Quiet Heart* (Ann Arbor, Mich.: Vine Books, Servant, 1995), 39.

CHAPTER 7: THE EAGLE'S ENEMIES
1. A. W. Tozer, *That Incredible Christian* (Camp Hill, Pa.: Christian Publications, 1986), 88.

Other titles from Moody Press:

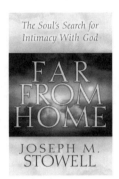

The reality of heaven is the cord that keeps pulling us onward and upward in life. Yet, if eternity is not the habit of our heart, life soon becomes hollow and unsatisfying. The frantic pace and seductiveness of this present world threaten to blur our focus on eternity. We are left with a nagging sense of meaninglessness that haunts our souls.

ISBN# 0-8024-4153-X

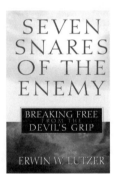

Opportunities to be ensnared by sin abound today. We live in a world filled with enticements that wait to trip us up and even reach out to us from the Internet, movies, television and the world at large in an effort to pull us into their grasp. Many good people, even Christians, are caught by these snares—and one wrong decision can start a progression that results in destroyed lives.

ISBN#0-8024-1164-9

For many Christians, God the Father seems as distant as Jesus seems reachable. We wonder about how the Father sees us, what He wants from us. We recognize that we understand very little about His character. But to really know Him seems impossible. Yet nothing could be further from the truth.

ISBN#0-8024-3007-4

Moody Press, a ministry of Moody Bible Institute,
is designed for education, evangelization, and edification.
If we may assist you in knowing more about Christ
and the Christian life, please write us without obligation:
Moody Press, c/o MLM, Chicago, Illinois 60610.